TRANSITION TO TWINS

Your First Multi-Engine Rating

TRANSITION TO TWINS

Your First Multi-Engine Rating

DAVID ROBSON

A Focus Series Book

Aviation Supplies & Acadamics, Inc

Newcastle, Washington

Transition to Twins: Your First Multi-Engine Rating
by David P. Robson

First published 1998 in Australia as *The Multi-Engine Piston* by the Aviation
Theory Centre Pty Ltd.

First ASA Edition 2000.

Aviation Supplies & Academics, Inc.
7005 132nd Place SE
Newcastle, Washington 98059-3153
Website: www.asa2fly.com
Email: asa@asa2fly.com

Nothing in this text supersedes any regulatory material or operational
documents issued by the Federal Aviation Administration or the aircraft
manufacturers or operators.

Published 2000 by Aviation Supplies & Academics, Inc.

Printed in the United States of America

09   08   07   06   05   7   6   5   4   3

ISBN 1-56027-414-X
      978-1-56027-414-8
ASA-TWINS

Library of Congress Cataloging-in-Publication Data

Robson, David.
    Transition to twins : your first multi-engine rating / David Robson.
        p.   cm.
    "A focus series book."
    ISBN 1-56027-414-X
    1. Twin-engine airplanes—Piloting. 2. Aeronautics—Examinations—Study guides. I. Title.
TL711.T85 R63 2000
629.132'52343—dc21   00-046931

Table of Contents

Preface

This book was written and first published to satisfy the needs of Australian and British pilots who were about to undergo their first endorsement (rating) on a multi-engine piston aircraft. It follows the sequence and meets the requirements of the licensing authorities and training organizations in those countries.

By popular demand, it has now been published in the U.S. and has been adapted for the U.S. operating environment. The principles do not change. However, the procedures and techniques advocated by the FAA may differ slightly. You should discuss these aspects with your flight instructor.

We recognized the need for more diverse study material that provides practical advice to newcomers to flying—whether on a professional or recreational basis. There is a wealth of knowledge that has been learned from the *school of hard knocks* that is not being widely disseminated. It relies on word of mouth. Some pilots have been lucky enough to rub shoulders with an old hand who had the wealth of experience and the desire to pass on the wisdom of years of learning. In our own way, we are trying to broaden the distribution of such wisdom. In doing so, we are very conscious that not all advice is black-and-white and that there are widely differing views on many topics. Aviation is still an art rather than a science. For this reason we are also vulnerable to criticism for synthesizing and interpreting many differing viewpoints.

We hope that the information contained in this manual is taken in the spirit in which it is given—as advice with which we take every care but for which the responsibility ultimately lies with the reader. We hope it will promote discussion and thought. Use it wisely.

David Robson

Author

David Robson is a career aviator having been nurtured on balsa wood, dope (the legal kind) and tissue paper. He made his first solo flight in a De Havilland Chipmunk shortly after his seventeenth birthday. He made his first parachute jump at the age of sixteen. His first job was as a junior draftsman (they weren't persons in those days) at the Commonwealth Aircraft Corporation in Melbourne, Australia. At the same time, he continued flying lessons with the Royal Victorian Aero Club. He joined the Royal Australian Air Force (RAAF) in 1965 and served for twenty-one years as a fighter pilot and test pilot. He flew over 1,000 hours on Mirages and 500 on Sabres (F-86 with a Rolls-Royce engine). He completed the Empire Test Pilot's course at Boscombe Down in England in 1972, flying everything from gliders, to the magnificent Hunter, Canberra and Lightning. He completed a tour in Vietnam with the United States Air Force, as a Forward Air Controller, flying the O 2A—*Oscar Deuce*. He was a member of the seven-aircraft formation aerobatic team, the *Deltas*, which flew his favorite aircraft, the Mirage fighter. This team was specially formed to celebrate the fiftieth anniversary of the RAAF.

After retiring from the Air Force, he became a civilian instructor and lecturer. During 1986-88 he was the editor of the *Aviation Safety Digest* which won the Flight Safety Foundation's international award. He spent over ten years at the Australian Aviation College as the Chief Instructor, Director of Pilot Training and Manager, Business Development. The college had 35 airplanes and trained over 1,000 cadet pilots for the world's leading airlines. In 1998, he was awarded the Australian Aviation Safety Foundation's Certificate of Air Safety. He loves airplanes, aerobatics and instructing—and he still dreams of, one day, flying a Spitfire.

Introduction

The title of this book encompasses a wide variety of aircraft. A multi-engine aircraft comes in many guises and many sizes. The main purpose of this book is to provide information and advice to pilots undergoing their first Multi-Engine Rating. It is less likely that this would be conducted in a three or four engine aircraft and engine failure in these or in a centerline thrust twin is less critical in terms of control or performance than a light twin. Our focus then is a conventional twin with wing-mounted engines and tractor propellers.

Why fly a twin-engine aircraft? There are basically two reasons to seek a multi-engine rating on your pilot's licence:

- you want the added performance and safety margins that are potentially offered by a multi-engine aircraft; or
- you are progressing up the rungs of the pilots' career ladder and the next stage of qualification and employment is the multi.

A twin-engine aircraft is the next stage of performance and complexity although many complex singles can offer equivalence. The real advantages of the twin are complete duplication, and therefore redundancy, of all systems—including the *spare* engine and propeller—in addition to the added performance over a similar technology single.

But it comes at a potential price—the consequences of an engine failure are less clear-cut and may be more difficult to handle than the single. This is not a major problem if the pilot is properly trained and maintains currency in practising for these circumstances.

Why have two engines—or are two better than one?

Two heads are better than one—but does this apply to engines? Statistically, you have a greater probability of a failure with a more complex aircraft but in practical terms, the consequences of that failure won't be as serious—if the pilot is properly trained and current. This is a significant proviso and is probably the major reason that licensing authorities don't demand that all aircraft have two or more engines. Modern engines are very reliable and the chances of surviving a forced landing are reasonable. The chances of an non-current pilot coping with an engine failure on takeoff in a twin are not so good. Similarly, many accidents occur on the final approach with one engine feathered—a situation that should be relatively under control. If you are properly trained and current, the procedures are not difficult. That's why you are here.

So, two are better than one, provided that the pilot is properly prepared and above all, never places the aircraft in a situation where the second engine cannot be used to get out of trouble. Otherwise there is no point having the second engine. This requires a depth of preflight planning that is well above that required for a single.

There are two aspects relating to engine failure:

- control; and
- performance.

The design category for light twins does not guarantee positive climb performance in all circumstances following engine failure. The *Queen of the Skies* is likely to become a *Drag Queen*.

Nevertheless, controllability comes first and this book highlights all of the factors that affect control following engine failure. It is significant that although twins suffer less accidents than singles, the twin accident is more serious.

The knowledge contained in this book is particularly important as it forms the basis for understanding the principles of multi-engine flying that apply to all subsequent types that you may fly. Having said that, there may be specific items not covered in this book or explained for a generic twin-engined aircraft, that are not applicable to your aircraft. Treat the contents of this book as advice and please follow the directives and instructions of your instructor and Flight Manual.

This manual will give you an understanding of the principles and practice of operating a twin. It is structured in two parts:
• Part One—general principles and procedures.
• Part Two—a suggested program for the multi-engine rating.

Please study this material and discuss it actively with your instructor until you are comfortable in the knowledge that you understand all aspects.

Flying a twin demands a professional attitude. You can fly a small single in a casual way and get away with it. Not so the twin. If you are not going to be able to keep abreast of the regulations and procedures and remain current on the aircraft, I would have second thoughts about converting to a twin.

There is much talk about human factors these days and they are not only applicable to the operation of heavy jets with two crew. The personal qualities of the pilot are just as important in the light, single pilot twin. Your instructor will have introduced the concept of *airmanship. Care in the air* is what it is all about and it will keep you and your passengers, alive. It includes also the quality of your decision-making. More about this later.

Welcome to the world of multi-engines, the next step on the ladder of professional pilotage.

Happy landings or, more importantly, happy takeoffs.

Chapter 1

Introducing the Twin and its Systems

Introduction

Where Are You Coming From?

The step up to a twin involves a significant change in complexity from the small single-engine aircraft in which you trained. Probably the best way to approach the twin is to firstly become familiar with the *complex* single, which has many systems in common with a typical twin. Then we will separately tackle the multi-engine aspects. Let's start with a brief look at the features of a typical complex single. The most noticeable features will be:

- retractable landing gear;
- electrically operated flaps;
- perhaps electrically operated elevator trim;
- rudder trim in addition to elevator trim;
- constant-speed propeller; and
- turbocharger on the engine.
  It could also have the following:
- IFR instrumentation, including an autopilot and, perhaps, weather radar;
- separate entrance for the passengers;
- air conditioning and, perhaps, pressurization;
- oxygen system; or
- several baggage compartments and a more complex loading system.

The principle of operation of these systems is well and truly described in the ASA-PM-2 and -3, *Private and Commercial* and *Instrument Flying* manuals, so let's concentrate on the practical implications and functioning of these systems.

Complex Systems

Retractable Landing Gear

The landing gear will be electrically selected. The normal extension and retraction will either be direct by an electric motor or indirect by an electrically driven hydraulic pump. There is little difference between them as far as the pilot is concerned. The hydraulic gear tends to be faster operating.

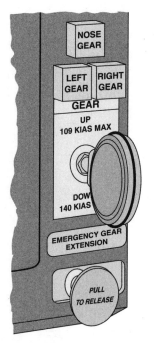

■ **Landing gear selector and lights**

There will be limiting speeds for operation of the gear (V_{LO}) and for flight with it extended (V_{LE}). There may even be one maximum speed for selecting the gear down and another maximum speed after takeoff by which the landing gear must be up. The Pilot's Operating Handbook will explain the particular limits for your aircraft.

The lights show green when the gear is down and locked, red when the gear is in transit, and go out when the wheels are up and locked. The gear will have a micro-switch on one leg, known as the *squat switch*, to prevent up selection when there is weight on the wheels. There will be a warning horn that operates when the throttles are retarded at low airspeed and the gear is up. It may also depend on flap position.

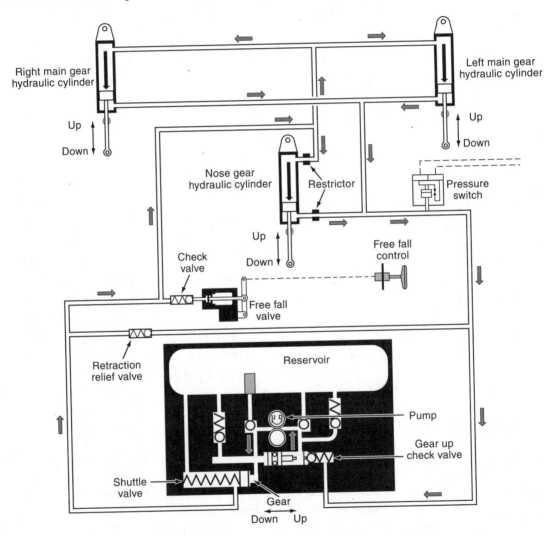

■ **Typical hydraulic retractable landing gear system**

There will be an emergency extension facility—either:
- a pressure dump and gravity drop of the gear (free fall);
- a manual handle to pump the gear down hydraulically; or
- a crank handle which will manually wind the gear down.

The manual crank may take 50–60 turns and may be difficult to operate while flying. Practice occasionally in VFR conditions.

With manual extension there may be no lights to indicate the landing gear is down and locked—but generally you can feel them extend and lock. (There may be a mirror on the side of the engine nacelle of the twin to visually check the extension of the nosewheel.)

Constant-Speed Propeller

The constant-speed propeller offers a much higher level of efficiency and, with it, some complication in its operation. Oil pressure is used to drive the blade angle, and a governor mechanism then controls the angle to maintain the selected RPM. Loss of oil pressure causes the blades to go to the full fine position. In addition to the RPM indicator, the pilot has a manifold pressure gauge (MP) with units of inches of mercury. Power is set by a combination of MP and RPM. The throttles control MP and the propeller levers, RPM. Typical settings are 25 in./2,500 RPM for climb and 23 in./2,300 RPM for cruise.

To avoid stress on the engine, MP should be less than RPM ÷ 100.

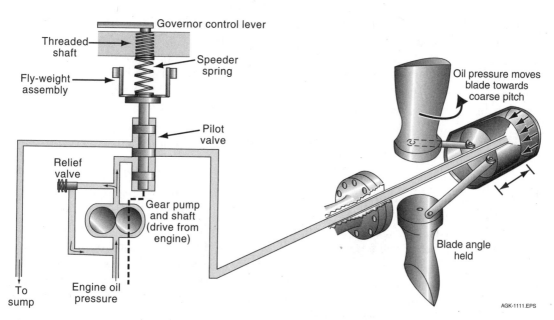

AGK-1111.EPS

■ **Constant speed propeller unit**

The levers have to be selected in a certain order (prop up before throttle and throttle back before RPM reduction—*revs up and throttle back*) to avoid the risk of detonation.

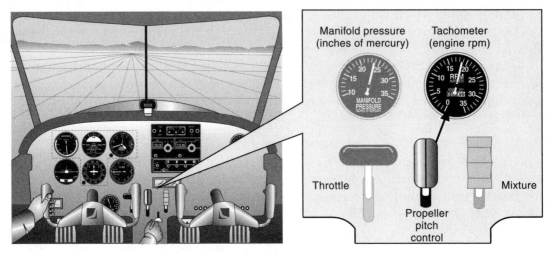

■ **Propeller rpm selector from cockpit**

Electric Flaps

Flaps could be manually or electrically operated by a simple switch with detents for *up*, *takeoff* and *land* positions. There is a sensor on the flaps to stop the electric motor when the flaps reach the selected setting (*select and forget*). There is a position indicator to show the actual position of the flaps. They are mechanically connected to prevent asymmetric positions. It is very valuable to be able to reach and select the various flap positions without having to look inside for the switch or to read the position indicator—except for confirmation. A little time spent in the cockpit rehearsing all checks is worthwhile. (Chuck Yeager learned his checks until he could do them blindfolded.)

Electric Trim

For the electric trim system, the usual cable-operated elevator trim has an electric motor to position both the trim tab and the trim wheel. (It is quite remarkable to watch the trim wheel in a Boeing aircraft spinning under the influence of the electric trim!) The trim switch will be on the control yoke to be operated by the thumb and it works in a conventional sense—forward for nose down trim and vice versa. The switch is spring-loaded to the central *off* position. The regulations require that the trim can be manually overridden or disconnected but be careful. In some aircraft, the out-of-trim forces can be so high as to interfere with safe operation of the aircraft—especially on takeoff when you need one hand to operate other controls.

Autopilot

The autopilot is a friend and a powerful one at that. It is your right hand, or more specifically, it frees your right hand to do other things. Having an autopilot to hold the wings level significantly reduces the cockpit work load for single pilot operations. During VFR navigation, day or night, keeping the wings level is more than half the battle. Even if you do not intend to fly your twin under IFR, the autopilot is a valuable aid and you should learn its modes of operation. The simple modes of *heading hold* and *altitude hold* are extremely useful. It is no disgrace to fly on autopilot.

A simple autopilot is *single-axis* (roll mode only), that is, it can maintain wings level or maintain a heading but has no pitch attitude nor altitude hold functions.

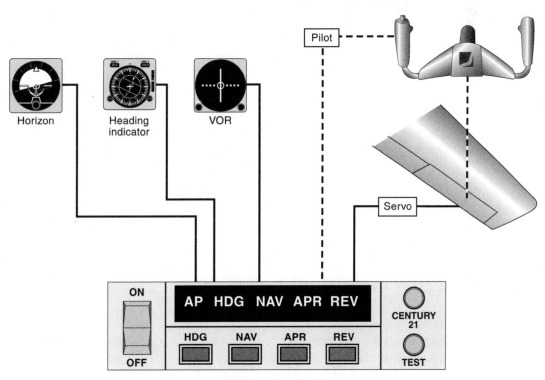

■ **Single axis autopilot**

A *two-axis* autopilot (roll and pitch modes) has attitude and altitude hold, navigation modes and a glideslope capability for the ILS. It will have a pitch wheel for the pilot to *trim* the attitude for level flight, climb or descent. More advanced autopilots also have airspeed hold.

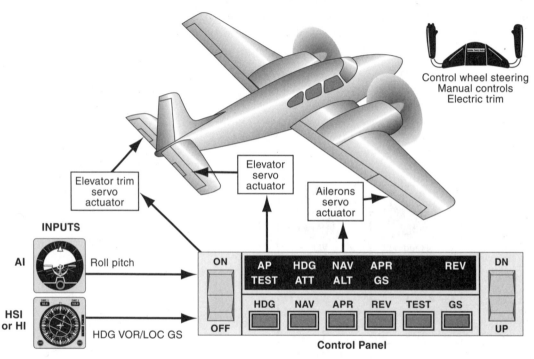

■ **Typical two-axis autopilot control and display panel**

The basic modes of operation are:

Heading Hold. Heading hold maintains the heading that is set on the *bug* on the heading indicator. The autopilot will also turn the aircraft to follow the heading bug when it is repositioned. When it is aligned, it maintains the wings level.

ALT. In the altitude mode, the autopilot will maintain or level off at the altitude at which it is engaged. However, it will maintain altitude even if there is not enough thrust to do so. Therefore airspeed can decay—be careful.

NAV. In the navigation mode the autopilot will follow the CDI bar of the VOR and therefore maintain the selected track, outbound or inbound, in a *command* sense.

Approach. In the approach mode the autopilot will intercept and maintain centerline of the localizer and will capture the glideslope when armed and within limits.

ATT. In the attitude hold mode it will maintain the selected attitude. It will also automatically adjust the electric elevator trim. The pilot can *fine-tune* the attitude with a small switch on the autopilot panel.

The autopilot will have manual select and deselect switches and a cut-out button on the control column. There will be specific preflight checks especially of the basic modes and the disconnect functions. The autopilot can be manually overridden by force and it will disconnect in the process. This is also checked before flight. There will be maximum airspeed and minimum altitudes which you must observe. Your autopilot is your useful friend. It is more important to know its functions than any other aid.

Heating and Air Conditioning

The typical heating system consists of a thermostat controlled, fuel-burning combustion heater in the nose of the aircraft, an electrically operated fan and ducting to the cabin outlets and the windscreen demist. It operates automatically when hot air is selected. Bear in mind that it is fuel consuming and it may be appropriate to include it in your fuel planning allowances. A heater in a light twin uses less than one U.S. gallon per hour (4.5 liters).

Air conditioning is equivalent to your motor vehicle and offers no additional function. It is separate to pressurization and is designed for use on the ground or at lower altitudes on a hot day. The air conditioner draws engine power and so must be off for takeoff and landing.

Navaids

It is assumed that you are already familiar with the navaids for your type of operation, (VFR or IFR) and are proficient in their use. If you wish to revisit their principles of operation and IFR procedures, ASA-PM-3, *Instrument Flying* manual, contains very detailed descriptions. But there is the central flight management system (FMS) to consider.

Central Processor or Flight Management System (FMS)

All functions of an aircraft and its systems are monitored and operated by the pilot in response to inputs he or she receives from external or internal cues.

In the case of the basic twin, the flight management system (FMS) is the pilot's brain and this has to adapt to the complexity, skills and knowledge required by the new environment. It has to *learn* the procedures and techniques associated with flying a twin.

As well as the increased total complexity of the aircraft and systems, there is another vital element of the transition from the single to the twin. This is the *rate-at-which-things-happen*. The mind needs time to adjust and to build in the necessary anticipation.

To go from a Cessna 150 to a Duchess is a big step, as it is from a Warrior to a Baron. It takes time for the brain to adjust to the new processor speed required. It takes another *32 MB of RAM* or a *Pentium III*, but you can't simply add a new card. You have to train the old one. Processing speed *can* be increased though. Some time in a high performance single to get the hands, feet and brain functioning at *retractable* speeds, before getting into the twin, is invaluable.

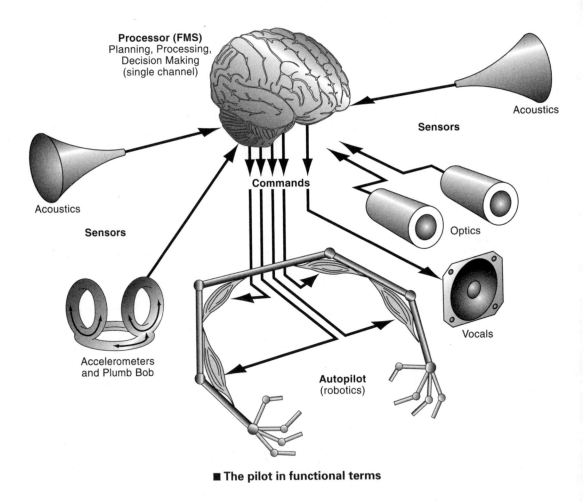

■ The pilot in functional terms

Time spent in the cockpit of your twin on the ground mentally rehearsing and re-living what you saw and did in the air is equally valuable.

Twins

Now that we are *up-to-speed* with a complex single, let's proceed to the twin.

A twin comes in many guises:

■ **Twins in many guises**

We will focus on the low-wing, conventional tail, retractable landing gear configuration, which is most common.

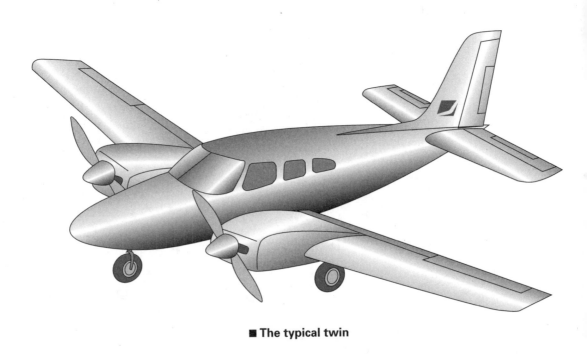

■ **The typical twin**

A *typical*, light, twin piston-engine aircraft will be significantly faster and heavier than your trainer and will have the following additional features:
- Two engines (fuel injected and perhaps turbocharged) with constant-speed, fully feathering propellers and cowl flaps on the nacelles. The propellers could be *handed*, that is a different direction of rotation between the left and right engines.
- Perhaps pressurization and oxygen.
- A complex fuel system with crossfeed.
- Dual electrical systems with two generators or alternators.
- Perhaps a second entry door and passenger compartment.
- Additional baggage lockers.
- Possibly a fire warning and extinguishing system.
- Possibly de-icing or anti-icing equipment.

Let's now *walk* around our twin and have a closer look at some of its features.

Fuel Injection

Fuel injection offers a more efficient and more powerful means of feeding the engine. It removes the carburetor and hence the need for carburetor heating but air for the fuel injection system passes through a filter and to ensure an adequate supply in the event of induction icing, there is an alternate air intake—not to be confused with the alternate static source for the pressure instruments. The selector for the alternate air is likely to be under the instrument panel as is the selector for the alternate static source. The alternate air is unfiltered and care needs to be taken in dusty conditions.

The fuel injectors supply metered amounts of fuel to gain optimum engine efficiency and power.

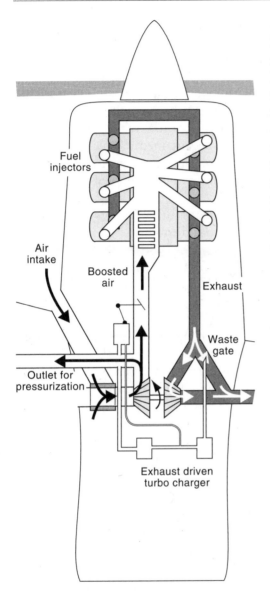

Fuel injectors

Air intake

Boosted air

Exhaust

Waste gate

Outlet for pressurization

Exhaust driven turbo charger

■ **A typical fuel injection system and turbocharger.**

The starting procedure for an injected engine will be a little different from the carbureted engine. It is usual to prime with the fuel pump on, the throttle open and mixture rich, and then to set the throttle, turn off the boost pump and select mixture to cut-off. The mixture goes back to full rich when the engine starts. Some engines can be temperamental and it is important to observe the start procedures for hot and cold conditions and hot or cold engines.

Turbochargers

The turbocharger, or supercharger in older aircraft, is a system for boosting or pressurizing the fuel-air mixture that is being supplied to the intake manifold. In the case of a turbocharger, it is driven by exhaust gases from the engine. The amount of pressurization is a balance between what the engine can cope with and the capacity of the turbo. Too much and the engine is overboosted and can be damaged. At higher altitudes, the engine can cope but the turbo cannot sustain the equivalent fuel-air mixture for full power, and above this *full throttle altitude*, maximum power cannot be sustained.

On a modern system there will be an automatic waste gate to adjust the turbo but on older systems, the pilot has to control it manually and has to be careful not to overboost the engine at lower altitudes.

Exhaust gas–driven superchargers are generally known as turbochargers because they are driven by a turbine running off the exhaust gas from the engine. The turbine in turn drives a centrifugal compressor.

Turbochargers have become very popular, especially in smaller engines, as they do not need the heavy and expensive gearing of the supercharger. Modern metallurgy and turbine design has made the turbocharger a reliable and reasonably efficient means of restoring power to engines at high altitudes.

The heart of the turbo is a very high speed turbine operating at very high temperatures. It is vulnerable to sudden changes in engine speed and temperature.

Control of the turbocharger is made through a waste gate which can spill the exhaust gas straight into the exhaust system when it is open, or, when closed, force all the gas to go through the turbine before entering the exhaust system, thus providing maximum power to the compressor.

Control of the waste gate varies with aircraft design but may be categorized as either:
- variable waste gate; or
- fixed waste gate.

The variable waste gate, as its name implies, is able to move from fully open (no turbocharging) to fully closed (full turbocharging.)

Generally three systems are used to vary the waste gate.
- A lever or second throttle operated by the pilot. When the normal throttle is fully open on climb the waste gate can be gradually closed to give more power as required. This gives the pilot more direct control over the engine but is a little more complicated to use.
- The waste gate can be connected directly to the throttle so that as the throttle is opened, the waste gate is closed and the turbocharger comes in. This is simpler to use but operators must be careful as a little movement of the throttle can give a big power increase.
- Automatic movement as needed and determined by sensors. This system is complex and expensive although probably the most efficient overall. Variable waste gate systems usually have a pressure relief valve to dump any overboosted air.

The fixed waste gate system is the simplest system although it has many drawbacks. This system has the waste gate at a set position (adjustable on the ground) and therefore the pilot does not have to worry about it. However, this means that at no stage is all the exhaust gas available to supply the turbine. Thus the amount of boost available at higher altitudes is limited. Similarly at low altitudes some turbocharging is in operation even though it is not needed. Because of this, care must be taken during takeoff and the early part of the climb as overboosting will occur if the throttle is fully opened.

With all types of turbochargers power changes should be smooth and anticipated, so the throttle movement is even slower than you were used to in the normally aspirated (normally breathing) single. Plan on four seconds from idle to full power and vice versa. The significant caution with turbochargers is thermal stress. They turn at an extremely high RPM and so cannot tolerate sudden temperature changes. The critical times are reducing power for a descent, simulating engine failures and stabilizing the temperature prior to shutdown. There will be a minimum run-down time where the engines are allowed idle for about two minutes, to stabilize the temperature before the engines are shutdown.

Fully Feathering Propeller

The significant differences between the constant-speed propeller and the fully feathering propeller are:
- the feathering propeller has a greater blade angle range beyond the full coarse position; and
- the loss of oil pressure causes the blades to go to the feathered (full coarse) position (rather than the fully fine position, as is the case in a single).

The propeller system may include an unfeathering accumulator. This device stores pressure energy to unfeather the propeller after practice asymmetric situations.

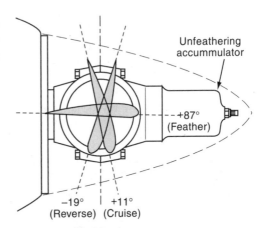

Unfeathering accummulator

+87° (Feather)

−19° (Reverse)   +11° (Cruise)

■ Blade angles of a fully feathering propeller

The system also incorporates a locking pin which prevents the propeller going to the feather position as the RPM decays and the oil pressure drops—that is, when the engine is shutdown. This pin is designed to operate at about 900 RPM, which is well below any in-flight range even when the propeller is windmilling (except engine seizure). The operation of the feathering propeller is straightforward and the same as the constant-speed propeller for normal operations. The feathered position is selected retarding the propeller RPM levers through low RPM range to the rear-most position. Note that the RPM setting is independent of throttle position and it is possible to feather the *live* engine.

Fuel System

The complexities of the fuel system of the twin have been the cause of many accidents. It is possible to incorrectly select fuel from empty tanks, to crossfeed to a failed engine, to suffer an engine failure due to fuel starvation (even though there are full tanks) and to consume all fuel from one side and none from the other.

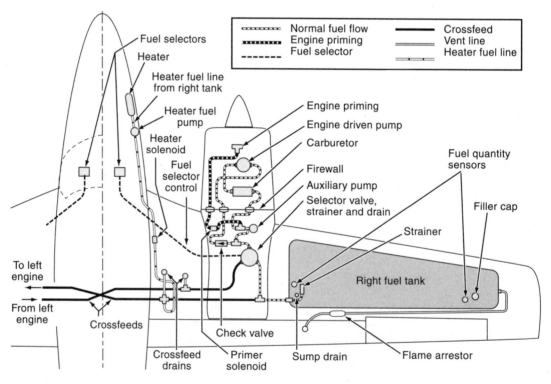

■ **A simple fuel system**

Typical fuel systems are illustrated here, but the one system that you must learn thoroughly is the fuel system for *your* aircraft.

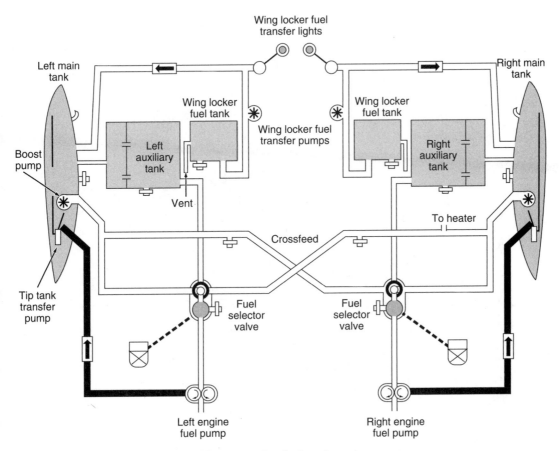

■ More complex fuel tank system

There will be limitations on the use of crossfeed (not to be used for takeoff for instance). Fuel should be off to the dead engine while crossfeeding the live engine. There will be a sequence for fuel transfer, use of boost pumps, and a preferred sequence for fuel feed from auxiliary tanks and ferry tanks. There will be procedures and restrictions on refuelling, fuel types and grades as well as vents and drains. You must know them all.

Pressurization System

With the larger twins the excess power of the engines can be diverted to other things such as driving a pressurization turbine. However, like your car's air conditioner it does draw power and must only be used when all engines are operating normally.

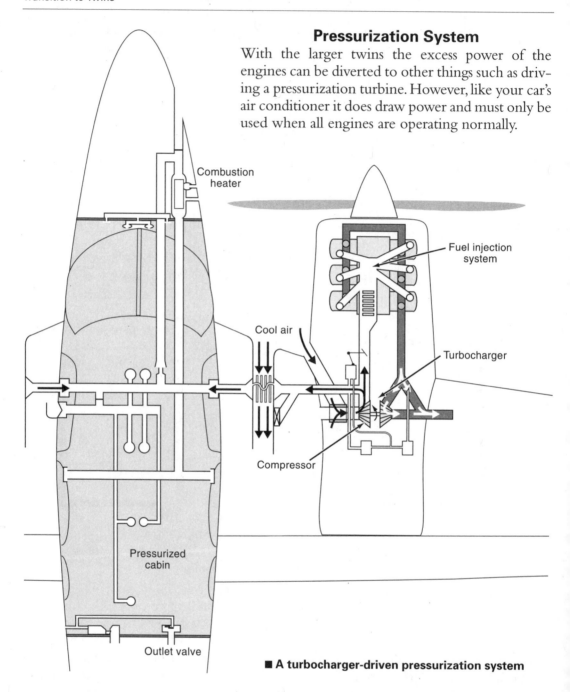

Combustion heater

Fuel injection system

Cool air

Turbocharger

Compressor

Pressurized cabin

Outlet valve

■ **A turbocharger-driven pressurization system**

Having said that, the pressurization system is designed so that the cabin pressure is supplied continuously from engine bleed air by the turbocharger or by a separate compressor.

The pressure of the cabin is adjusted by controlling the outlet valve at the rear of the bulkhead. In this way, once the cabin is pressurized, it is maintained for a reasonable amount of time in the event of engine failure. Usually, one engine can sustain the selected cabin pressure but check your aircraft for particular requirements and limitations. The outlet valve maintains a preset pressure differential (the difference between the cabin

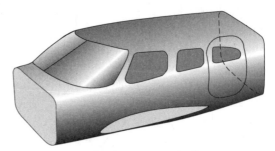

■ **Cabin pressure hull**

pressure and outside air pressure). It also acts as a safety valve to prevent over-pressure. Normally 4-5 psi is a maximum. It is usual to refer to pressure levels as equivalent altitudes—i.e. cabin altitude or aircraft altitude. The system is not fully automatic though. The pilot sets the aircraft's altitude plus 500 ft before takeoff. At cruise altitude the pressure regulator will maintain the maximum allowable differential but will cycle as the pressure builds and is released. If you set cruise altitude plus 500 ft this uncomfortable cycling can be avoided.

Typically the pilot will turn the pressurization on after engine start. The pressurization seal around the door inflates automatically. During the climb, the pressure differential will increase and the cabin altitude will remain at sea level until the limit of 4 psi is reached. The cabin altitude will then *climb* as the aircraft climbs. The differential of 4 psi gives a cabin altitude of 8,000 ft with an aircraft altitude of 35,000 ft and a cabin altitude of sea level up to an aircraft altitude of 25,000 ft. Before descent, the pilot selects the destination circuit altitude plus 500 ft. As the aircraft descends, the cabin will also descend until the cabin reaches sea level, i.e. the cabin *lands* before the aircraft. The cabin altitude must never be higher than the aircraft altitude. The pilot can manually control cabin *rate of descent*. Also the regulator will not allow *negative* pressure. On landing, a *squat* switch will open the valve and dump any residual pressure. It is also good practice to open your side window before opening the cabin door to avoid possible injury to people outside.

Oxygen System

As you fly at higher altitudes, you are entering a regime where the human body will not survive without assistance—in this case supplemental oxygen. The thinner air at these altitudes does not provide sufficient oxygen to maintain normal human functions. Eventually, there are risks of visual impairment and loss of consciousness. For the average human, the research doctors have produced tables of *times of useful consciousness* which show the expected period during which you can expect to function reasonably at different altitudes. The oxygen system is a *critical to maintain* and *critical to operate* system and the individual operation of your system must be understood before flying above 10,000 feet. If you require a quick-donning oxygen mask, check that you can fit it quickly and consistently. Effects of hypoxia are insidious and your particular response can be experienced in a decompression chamber. It is valuable to be aware of your symptoms if you are going to fly regularly at higher altitudes.

Electrical System

The electrical system of a twin at first appears complex but basically consists of *bus bars* which are energized by both alternators. A bus bar is simply a device which distributes the electrical energy to various services. If one engine or alternator fails, the bus bar is still sustained by the live alternator although some loads may have to be shed. In some aircraft, the system incorporates an automatic load shedding bus which disconnects non-essential or less important electrical services in the event of reduced electrical power.

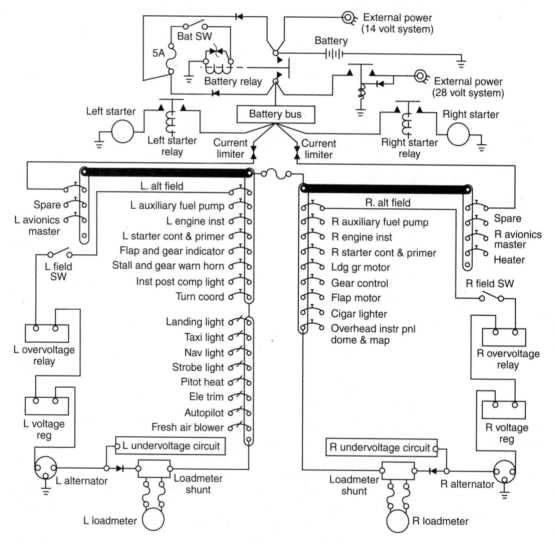

■ **Typical duplex electrical system**

The critical times are when one engine or alternator fails and you need services which require a substantial load such as the landing light, demist fans or blowers, pitot heat and flaps. Fortunately, the absolutely essential services of flight instruments, navaids and comms require little electrical current and can generally be maintained. Discuss with your instructor what services should be turned off under these circumstances. Don't use the cigarette lighter!

De-icing and Anti-icing Systems

Anti-icing systems prevent ice build-up. De-icing systems shed ice. The twin will have at least pitot heat, carb heat, hot air windscreen demist and perhaps windscreen wipers. There will be alternate air intakes for the turbochargers.

Aircraft designed for operation in icing conditions, will also have inflatable rubber *de-icing boots* on the wing and horizontal stabilizer leading edges and perhaps electrically heated windscreen and propellers. Some use liquid de-icing.

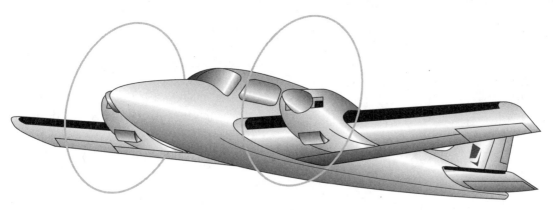

■ **De-icing boots**

De-icing boots inflate and deflate in a controlled cycle and should only be used after the ice has hardened to cause it to crack and be blown away. If they are cycled when the ice particles are just building, they will form a hard shell over the space in which the boots cycle.

Fire Detection and Engine Fire Extinguishers

In some light twins there will be a continuous wire fire detection system which triggers a fire warning in the cockpit if the wire is burned through or broken. Some more complex aircraft also have fire extinguishers in the engine compartments.

A typical system consists of two heat sensors located in the engine compartment, a compressed gas, single-shot fire bottle located in the wheel well and two annunciator/actuators located on the annunciator panel.

When the annunciator panel *press to test* button is pressed, the fire warning lights should illuminate. During normal operation, if an overheat condition should occur, the applicable fire warning light will illuminate and a bell will sound. Lifting the clear plastic cover guard and pressing the red fire annunciator will close the bleed air and fuel firewall shutoff valves, disable the generator and arm the fire extinguishing system.

Pressing the white fire bottle armed light will discharge the fire extinguisher contents into the engine compartment. After the engine compartment cools, the red fire warning light will extinguish.

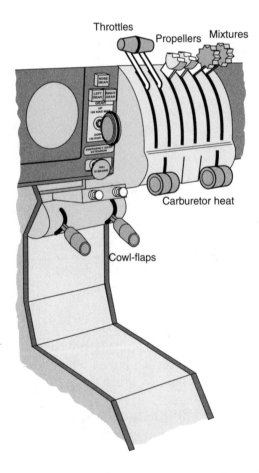

■ **Typical quadrant or center console**

Cockpit

It is in the cockpit that the differences between a single and a twin are even more significant.

The twin has:
- *doubled* throttles, mixtures, propeller levers, carburetor heat (unless fuel injected) and cowl–flap levers;
- a proper *quadrant* for the engine controls;
- *doubled* engine instruments or doubled needles on each;
- *doubled* ammeters or alternator lights;
- *doubled* starter switches and magneto switches (perhaps separate);
- more complex fuel system selectors with crossfeed;
- rudder trim and perhaps aileron trim as well as the usual elevator trim;
- fire warning lights; and
- an airspeed indicator with more lines, color coding and perhaps a *bug* or two to highlight reference airspeeds.

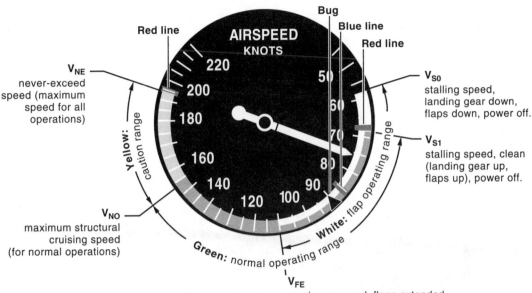

TYPICAL INDICATOR MARKINGS

Markings	IAS value or range Knots	Significance
White Line	60 - 110	Full Flaps Operating Range
Blue Line	85	Single-Engine Best-Rate-of-Climb
Red Line	65	Minimum Single-Engine Control (VMC)
Green Arc	70 - 154	Normal Operating Range
Yellow Arc	154 -194	Operate with Caution Only in Smooth Air
Red Line	194	Maximum Speed For All Operations (*Never Exceed*)

■ **Typical airspeed indicator markings**

It may have a hand–held microphone. If it has, throw it away or regard it as *emergency use only*. The workload in a twin does not allow for the fumbling of a microphone and does not offer the luxury of a spare hand with which to do it. Use a headset for yourself and your passengers. It protects their hearing, allows them to hear the Air Traffic Control instructions (they know when you are too busy to talk, especially if you explain your call-sign) and you can communicate with them in a normal voice. There have been many instances where the passengers have heard calls that the pilot missed and they have spotted conflicting traffic in time to warn the pilot.

Hypothetical Twin

For the purposes of illustration we have created a hypothetical twin-engine aircraft, the Bushcraft 71, which represents a typical 14 CFR Part 23 light twin.

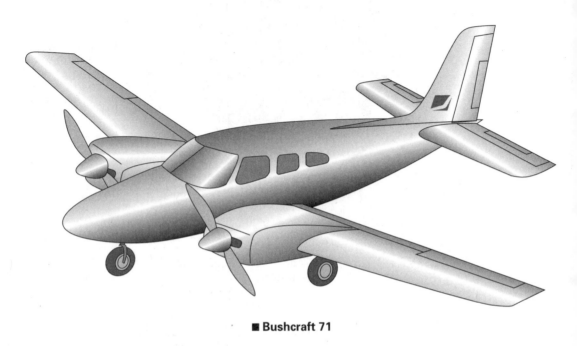

■ **Bushcraft 71**

We will use its representative speeds, attitudes, power weights and performance to indicate features and limitations inherent in a typical light twin.

So that's our twin. *Let's go flying!*

Chapter 2

Definitions

Before we embark on the multi-engine rating, we need to clarify the internationally accepted terminology for operation of multi-engine aircraft.

Speeds

V_{REF} The term used by airlines for the airspeed to achieve on short final. It is the reference airspeed and they use V_{REF} + 5, V_{REF} + 10 or V_{REF} + 15 at various stages of the approach. V_{REF} is factored on stalling speed ($1.3 \times V_{SO}$) and so varies with weight.

V_{AT} The target threshold speed is the last look speed you wish to see when you start the flare to land. V_{AT} is based on V_{REF} but can also include allowances for wind, gusts and turbulence.

V_Y The indicated airspeed for best rate of climb (greatest altitude in shortest *time*), all engines operating.

V_{YSE} The airspeed for best rate of climb, single-engine and also varies with weight although the manufacturer in the case of light twins, may simply quote the maximum weight case. For the larger aircraft with a broader range of weights, check for a variation in recommended V_{YSE} with gross weight.

Blue line The marking on the airspeed indicator corresponding to V_{YSE} at maximum weight.

V_X The airspeed for best angle of climb (greatest altitude in shortest *distance*), all engines operating.

V_{XSE} The airspeed for best angle of climb, single engine.

V_{SO} The stalling speed in the landing configuration with landing gear and flap down, power off.

V_{S1} The stalling speed, power off with landing gear and flaps up.

V_{LE} The maximum speed with the landing gear extended.

V_{LO} The maximum speed with the landing gear in transit (may be different going up/going down).

V_{FE} The maximum speed with the flaps extended and may vary for different flap settings.

V_{NO} The maximum speed for normal operations, in smooth air. It is known as the maximum structural cruising speed.

V_{NE} The speed that must *never* be exceeded, under any circumstances.

V_{MC}	The minimum control speed, airborne, under specified conditions. This is discussed in some detail later.
V_{MCG}	The minimum control speed on the ground and assumes the aircraft is continuing the takeoff. It is not applicable to light twins.
V_{MCL}	The minimum control speed in the landing configuration.
V_A	The speed at or below which the airframe cannot be overstressed by control deflection or turbulence. Its significance is that it is proportional to stalling speed and so varies with weight — the heavier the aircraft, the higher the value of V_A. It is also known as the maximum maneuvering speed.
TOSS	Takeoff safety speed is a nominal speed factored to give a margin above both the stalling speed and minimum control speed. Thus it is the speed above which the aircraft is safely controllable. However, it does not guarantee any climb performance.
V_{SSE}	Safe single engine speed is a speed above V_S and V_{MC}, factored to provide a greater safety margin for deliberate asymmetric operations and training.
V_1	The speed at which it is still possible to stop in the remaining distance of the runway and stopway and beyond which the aircraft is committed to continue despite engine failure. This is significant for 14 CFR Part 25 or higher performance aircraft that have a guaranteed performance after an engine failure. It is not so applicable for the light twin as under some circumstances, it may be better to run off the end of the runway than lose control after lift off (or have to descend and land further on).
V_2	Takeoff safety speed as used by operators of larger aircraft including military. It is factored for V_S and V_{MC}.
V_R	The speed at which the aircraft is rotated to the takeoff attitude for lift off.
V_{IMD}	The indicated airspeed for minimum drag.

Other Definitions

Density Altitude

Density altitude is pressure altitude modified by temperature. It reflects the density of the air and therefore airframe and engine performance.

Aborted Takeoff

A takeoff that is aborted, terminated or discontinued. Abort is the more common term. An aborted landing is called a go-around or under IFR, a missed approach.

Asymmetric

Asymmetric means non symmetrical or not the same. Thus any difference in thrust, drag or even fuel quantity from one wing to the other, is asymmetric. However, the term is generally used for real or simulated engine failure in a twin.

Power vs Thrust

Thrust is simply the amount of *push* that the engine/propeller is delivering. It is directly opposite to drag. Asymmetric thrust determines controllability and excess thrust determines instantaneous acceleration and angle of climb. Power is the *rate* of doing work (how fast) and so involves time. It is literally thrust × true airspeed and determines *rate* of climb and *rate* of fuel consumption. It is discussed in more detail later.

Service Ceiling

Service ceiling is the maximum altitude at which the aircraft can maintain a rate of climb of 100 ft per minute. The single-engine service ceiling is the maximum altitude for 50 fpm ROC on one engine, with the propeller of the failed engine feathered.

Absolute Ceiling

Absolute ceiling is that altitude at which the rate of climb on full power is reduced to zero and again it has a single-engine equivalent. Obviously it is wise not to plan a route that includes terrain above the single-engine absolute ceiling — just in case. Bear in mind also that to turn at absolute ceiling, involves accepting a rate of descent.

Stopway

Stopway is a defined rectangular area on the ground at the end of a runway in the direction of takeoff designated and prepared by the Airport Authority as a suitable area in which an aircraft can be stopped in the case of an interrupted takeoff.

Flight Level (FL)

The aircraft's cruising level to the nearest 500 ft above a standard pressure datum (29.92 inches of mercury). For example, with a setting of 29.92 in. Hg, an altimeter reading of 24,500 ft is stated as Flight Level 245 and 24,000 is FL 240. A pressure altimeter calibrated in accordance with the Standard Atmosphere:

- when set to local sea level pressure altimeter setting, will indicate altitude above sea level; and
- when set to a pressure of 29.92 is used to indicate Flight Level.

Transition Altitude

The altitude at or below which the cruising level of an aircraft is referenced to altitude above MSL.

Transition Layer

The airspace between the transition altitude and transition level.

Transition Level

The flight level at or above which the vertical position of an aircraft is controlled by reference to flight levels (29.92 is set).

Visual Approach Slope Indicator (VASI)

A system of lights arranged to provide visual information to pilots of their position in relation to the preset approach slope.

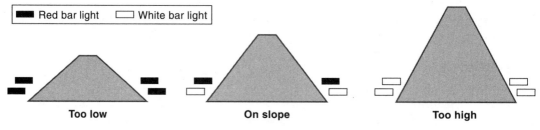

■ Red bar light	□ White bar light

Too low   **On slope**   **Too high**

■ **Perspectives on approach using a two-bar VASI**

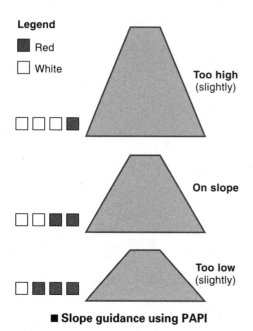

Legend

■ Red

□ White

Too high
(slightly)

On slope

Too low
(slightly)

■ **Slope guidance using PAPI**

PAPI (Precision Approach Path Indicator)

An approach aid consisting of four light boxes laterally positioned by the aim point. The number of lights change from white to red progressively as the aircraft moves from above to below glidepath. PAPI can be on either or both sides of the runway. PAPI indications can only be used for one designated aim point.

Chapter 3

Normal Operation of a Light Twin

Preflight Preparation

You need to be better prepared for a flight in a twin because the cockpit workload is higher, especially during your conversion. Time spent reading the procedures and sitting in the aircraft is priceless and is free. It is invalid to say that there isn't time to do this as you would otherwise waste time in the air and have to pay for it.

It is also valuable to practice and learn the in-flight checks for normal and abnormal operations. The written *challenge and response* checklist is fine if you have another crew member but alone, you don't need the added distraction of trying to read the items. The checklist is designed so that you do the checks first. Even the airline crews know their cockpit *cycles* and *do* the actions from memory before they *check* the items from the checklist.

Have your documentation ready and refamiliarize yourself with local procedures and radio calls. You should be able to concentrate on your flying and not have doubts about what you should be saying. Be early and expect a comprehensive briefing about the flight.

Preflight Inspection

The preflight inspection is routine but it is a good opportunity to get to know the aircraft. Note the propellers and their direction of rotation, the cowl flaps, baggage compartments, fuel filler caps and drain points. Have a look in the engine compartments and ask about the turbochargers, alternators and fire extinguishers.

Cockpit Checks

In the cockpit, confirm the operation of the fuel selectors, cowl flaps and emergency landing gear extension. Position your seat and if available, adjust it vertically to the design eye point. Ensure that you can apply full rudder deflection and that the seat is securely locked. Then carry out the recommended pre-start checks for your aircraft.

If there is only one entry door on the right hand side, leave it partly open for the start of the left engine and then be

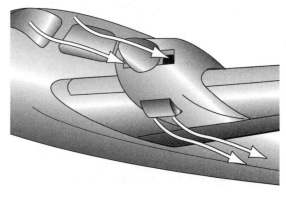

■ **Cowl flaps**

doubly sure that it is securely closed for the start of the right engine.

Starting Engines

It is usual to start one engine at a time—even if you have external electrical power. If possible, start the left engine first as you can see that the area is clear, and once the left engine starts, anyone in the area will assume the right is about to. The only exception would be if you only had one alternator (on the right engine) in which case you may need its electrical power to start the left engine.

Navigation lights or beacon should be turned on—but not strobe lights. Ensure the area is clear, shout *"Clear Prop!"* and start the left engine. You may start on battery. Equally, this may be the first time you have started the engine using external power.

When you come to start the second engine be doubly sure that you have the correct starter engage switch selected and that the magneto switch is on. Close and lock the right-hand door and start the right engine.

External Power

You also have an option of using an external battery cart or ground power unit for starting. These procedures are in your Pilot's Operating Handbook and usually involve special requirements for switch selections. Remember that it is your responsibility to ensure that the operator of the external power source is familiar with the operation and the signals you will use. Check the location of the external power and talk to the crewman about the start procedure and signals.

If you have ground crew in the area and in particular, if the connector for the external power is near one of the engines, or the nose, start with chocks in place and use a start sequence to avoid any need for the crewman to be close to the propeller arc. In some cases, e.g. the Piper Seminole, you have to shut down the right engine to have the external power disconnected and then restart.

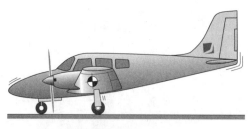

■ **The propeller clearance is reduced, particularly when braking**

Taxiing

The twin-engine aircraft has more mass than you are used to and so will require more thrust to get moving. Don't be harsh or hurried. You will generate a substantial slipstream so look out for smaller aircraft and people behind. Move both throttles as one and as the aircraft starts to move, reduce thrust and check the brakes. Taxiing is normal but requires some extra attention because of the increased wing-span. You will have an excellent forward view as there is no engine and propeller in the way.

The aircraft will tend to sway over bumps and around corners as there is more mass in the wings due to the engine nacelles and fuel tanks. It will give a softer ride for the same reason. There will be less vibration and as the engine mount is not next to your feet, there will be less engine noise. Propeller clearance in some twins is marginal so be cautious about bumps and soft or uneven ground, particularly when braking.

Because of the increased mass, there is extra distance needed for braking and although the brakes are designed to cope, it is important not to let the speed build up. Remember the energy to be dissipated is a function of the mass of the aircraft times the *square* of the speed—(double the speed, four times the kinetic energy).

Taxiing in High Winds—Use of Differential Thrust

A nice subtlety of taxiing a twin is the ability to set differential thrust on the engines so that the aircraft taxies straight in a crosswind. It is not difficult and it significantly reduces the need for differential braking. Be careful to avoid using thrust against partial braking. Hot brakes lose their effectiveness and they may be needed for an aborted takeoff.

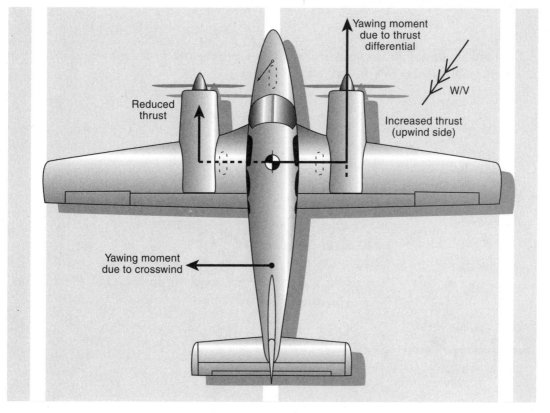

■ **Differential thrust to counter crosswind**

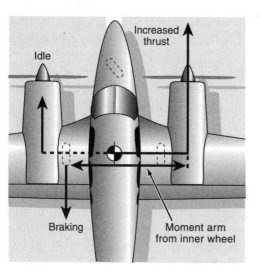

■ Using thrust, steering and braking

Maneuvering in Tight Spaces

Again the use of differential thrust offers significant improvements in the ability to maneuver in a tight space—especially effective with a touch of brake as the thrust line has a longer moment arm—but don't stop the inner wheel. However, if you have already applied full rudder deflection and perhaps some differential braking be careful not to place too great a side load on the nosewheel strut.

Caution: Don't stop the inner wheel as it will scrub the tread off the tire and may cause it to deflate. It can also roll the tire off the wheel.

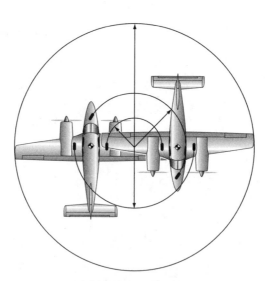

■ Minimum radius turn

On some twins the nosewheel strut is long and slender and does flex if the nosewheel is dragged sideways by differential braking or thrust. Always keep the inner wheel moving forward.

Emergency Stop

If the need arises, the twin can be stopped fairly quickly and in some aircraft, the parking brake applies full and immediate pressure to both brakes.

Shut down the engines if there is the slightest risk of collision or if there is a risk that the props could strike the ground.

Run-up And Pre-takeoff Checks

In the run-up area, stop the aircraft and apply the parking brake. The run-up checks in a twin are crucial and should neither be rushed nor abbreviated. There will be the usual checks for engine and systems but also a comprehensive check of the crossfeed system (at least on the

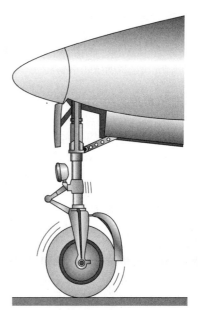

■ **Avoid side-loads when turning in a confined space**

first flight of the day) and the feathering of the propellers. Make sure that the fuel selectors are returned to *on* as takeoff is generally prohibited with crossfeed selected. For this reason carry out run-up checks before and separate from pre-takeoff vital actions. Run-up the engines individually. Do not fly an aircraft with a magneto drop that is out of limits. Similarly, if there is any significant difference in MP, fuel pressure or throttle position for the same RPM, have it checked.

It is preferable to run-up pointing into wind if your airport procedures allow it. There are considerable side loads and out-of-balance forces placed on an engine and propeller by running-up in crosswinds. You can actually hear and feel it. Also, run forward sufficiently to straighten the nosewheel before stopping.

Don't forget that you now have three trims to check. Double check that you can apply full rudder and that the seat is locked. Your life depends on it. Especially follow the autopilot and the fuel system checks.

Takeoff Safety Brief

The pre-takeoff safety brief is vital—even if you are alone. It helps because it brings into clear focus your pre-planned actions in the event of an emergency. Say them aloud so you can hear yourself stating your intentions.

The basis for the decision point and decision speed varies with runway length, obstacle clearance and aircraft category.

Given that you had selected the decision point, a typical safety brief, VFR might be something like this:

If the aircraft is still on the ground and an emergency occurs, I will abort the takeoff by closing the throttles, calling aborting, maintaining the runway centerline and braking. I will bring the aircraft to a complete stop, apply the parking brake and carry out the emergency drills. If there is a smell of smoke or signs of fire, I will evacuate the passengers and shut down the aircraft. I will advise the tower or UNICOM if the runway is occupied or, if safe, I will taxi clear of the runway.

If AOK, I will lift off at the recommended speed but delay landing gear retraction until I pass the decision point (or decision speed). If an engine fails before the decision point, I will close both throttles, lower full flap, land and brake as best I can to stop on the runway.

If I have selected the landing gear up, and there is an engine failure, I will prevent the yaw, hold a level attitude, accelerate to Blue Line (V_{YSE}) and identify the failure. I will then confirm the engine and feather the propeller.

High ground is on the left and so if I cannot maintain runway heading, I will turn right. If I cannot maintain altitude or airspeed, I will select a field visible in the windscreen and I will land ahead.

If you are clear in your mind before the event and you say the options and consequences *aloud*, it is more likely that your subconscious will register the procedure and you will instinctively react quickly and correctly, when the time comes. It is indecision that causes confusion, delayed reactions and incorrect actions. You must be *pro*active rather than *re*active.

I know this is an all-engines takeoff but what if the engine actually fails? This is not a simulated takeoff. It is a real one so be ready.

Also don't regard this brief as an exercise for the instructor's benefit. This brief is for *you*. It is *you* deciding and confirming what *you* will do.

Holding Point

Complete the last chance and holding point checks (landing light, pitot heat and transponder on) and self reminder of decision point/speeds and emergency actions.

10-Second Review

Having completed the before takeoff checklist, and prior to lining up on the runway for takeoff, it is good airmanship to conduct a 10-second review of:
- the wind direction (look at the windsock);
- the departure route if the takeoff is normal (initial heading and altitude);
- takeoff performance airspeeds (V_{MC}, lift off speed, speed at 50 ft, V_{SSE}, V_{YSE}, and V_Y);
- the expected takeoff distance and lift off point;
- the decision point or decision altitude at which to raise the landing gear (when a straight-ahead landing on the runway is no longer possible);
- relevant emergency procedures (such as engine failure during or after takeoff); and
- any expected radio frequency change after takeoff.
  With another pilot in the cockpit, this review must be spoken aloud.

Normal Takeoff

The normal takeoff is similar to a single. Consider both throttles as one. Taxi to the centerline and run forward until the nosewheel is straight. Stop. Then advance the throttles to half way—about 20 in. (static pressure is 30 in.)—and check both are indicating normally and the same. Then release the brakes and advance both throttles to full power.

Keep your hand over all levers but ready to close both throttles to abort if necessary. (You haven't yet reached the GO point.) Look outside at the center of the far end of the runway and keep straight. The acceleration will be greater than you are used to. (Since most twins can maintain altitude or climb on one engine then effectively the other engine is available for excess thrust and that determines acceleration). Have a quick look inside (check max RPM), check the temperatures and pressures are green and that the ASI is reading and then concentrate on keeping straight. As you reach rotate speed, apply steady back pressure and be ready for the aircraft to lift off. Maintain your initial climb attitude and allow the aircraft to accelerate. Keep your hand on the throttles and don't retract the landing gear until you are past the decision point. By then, you should have reached and passed Blue Line. Select landing gear up. You are now committed to continue.

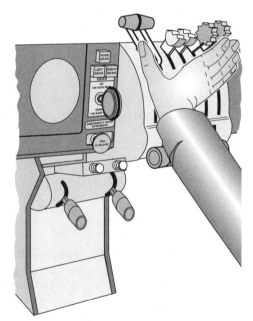
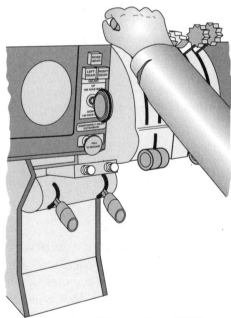

■ **Hand position ready to GO**   ■ **Hand position ready to STOP**

Place your hand across all power levers holding them fully forward to GO. Accelerate through V_{YSE} to V_Y. At V_Y and above 200 ft, retract the flaps, set climb power and adjust the climb attitude to maintain V_Y. Maintain wings level. Leave full power set until 500 ft, then reduce to climb power, turn off the boost pumps individually with a pause between. Busy period isn't it?

Leaning of Engines on Takeoff

Above density altitudes of 5,000 ft or more, some manufacturers recommend leaning the mixture for takeoff. *Check the manufacturer's recommendations.*

Crosswind Takeoff

The crosswind takeoff is similar to the normal takeoff with the use of *into wind* aileron during the ground roll. Positively rotate at V_R *plus* and allow the aircraft to weathervane into wind. (Imagine if you were to have an engine failure of the upwind engine at this point!). Maintain wings level and continue as for the normal takeoff. You can use differential thrust as you start to roll but make sure full power is set on both as soon as the rudder is effective.

Short-field Takeoff

The short-field takeoff should only be used when absolutely essential for obstacle clearance. Realize that the aircraft is very vulnerable during the period it is climbing at V_X (V_X is typically $1.1 \times V_{S1}$—and V_{MC} is typically not much higher). The aircraft is marginally above the stall and obstacles usually have associated turbulence. Engine failure during this phase requires lowering the nose and reducing power on the live engine to maintain control. Therefore the obstacle clearance will be non-existent. In the old days, this segment was called the *dead man's zone*. In my opinion, there should be no such thing as a short-field takeoff in a twin. If the runway meets the manufacturer's field length requirements and the obstacle clearance gradients meet the approach and takeoff requirements, there should be no need to do anything other than the safer, normal takeoff.

Climb

After takeoff and established in the climb attitude with climb power set, you can now relax a little and enjoy the performance offered by your twin. There are three climb profiles:
- maximum angle;
- maximum rate (normal); and
- cruise climb.

Unless there is a need to clear obstacles or to gain altitude quickly, use the cruise climb.

The reduced power, lower nose attitude and higher airspeed, provides lower stresses, improved cooling of the engines, better forward field-of-view, better passenger comfort and lower cabin noise levels. A typical initial climb attitude is +7° (7° nose-up).

Cruise

The noticeable aspect of the twin is the improved view during the cruise—there is nothing in front of you! Consequently, there is a tendency to be casual about attitude selection. Don't be tempted to fly performance instruments. Set an attitude, hold it, trim the aircraft and then check the instruments. You will generally be cruising at higher altitudes than you are used to so there is a need to manage the mixture controls.

Once normal cruise power is set, the cowl flaps can be retracted.

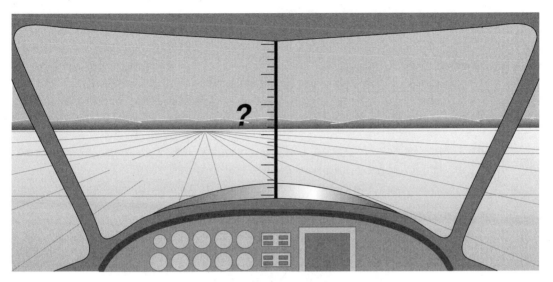

■ **Precise attitude reference**

Engine And Propeller Synchronization (SYNC)

If the propellers are out of *sync*, there is a *beat* or variation in sound like wowowowo which changes to wwowwowwowwoww to wowwwwwwowwwwowwwowwww and to wwwwwwwwwwww when they are in sync. To manually synchronize the engines, set both engines to the desired throttle and RPM settings by reference to the instruments. Then slowly advance the right throttle and note whether there is a harmonic oscillating sound and whether the frequency gets faster or slower. If faster, move the throttle slowly back and monitor the sound. After a while you should detect when the oscillation smooths to a continuous hum and then the engines are in sync.

If two propellers are rotating at slightly different RPMs, there may be some rhythmic vibration in the airframe. The number of beats per minute will be the same as the RPM difference. If, for instance, the left propeller is rotating at 2,400 RPM and the right propeller at 2,430 RPM, you will hear 30 audio beats per minute, which is one beat every 2 seconds. With 2,400 RPM and 2,410 RPM, you will hear 10 audio beats per minute, one every 6 seconds. The audio beats and the rhythmic vibration of the airframe can be very annoying.

With 2,400 RPM on the left engine and 2,430 RPM on the right engine, the audio beats will reduce progressively as you gently retard the propeller control of the *slave* right propeller. The beat frequency will reduce from 30 per minute, to 10, and then to zero when the two RPMs are identical. However, the instruments are not exact and only provide a guide to synchronization.

If you retard the right propeller control too far, and the two actual RPMs are 2,400 and 2,395, you will hear 5 beats per minute, one every 12 seconds. Move the slave control in the direction that reduces the beating.

Most twins have an optional electrical synchronizer or "Synchrophaser"—as it is sometimes called. Set the throttles and RPM as above and when the RPMs are within 20 or so switch on the sync. The automatic system slaves the right engine to the left and will maintain synchronization. However, if you wish to change power settings you have to disengage the auto sync, set the new RPM and manifold pressure and re-engage the auto-sync when it all stabilizes.

Three Axis Trimming

The correct sequence for trimming is to maintain a constant attitude and trim in pitch (hold the attitude constant while using the elevator trim wheel to remove any residual push or pull force).

Maintain the wings level with aileron and balance the aircraft with rudder. Then use the rudder trim to cancel any foot forces. Lastly, use the aileron trim to remove any residual lateral force. Be precise with attitude.

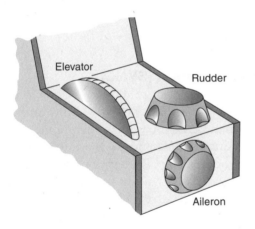

Remember:
- Change.
- Check.
- Hold.
- Adjust.
- *Trim.*

■ **Three axis trim wheels**

General Handling

Maneuver the twin through a few level turns, reversals, and climbing and descending turns. You will find that it has a higher inertia in roll—that is to say, that it is reluctant to start rolling and when it does, it is reluctant to stop. This is because of the greater mass in the wings. You will quickly get used to it and you will appreciate that the same mass distribution results in a better ride in turbulence. Also, the greater wing-span and the greater wing area cause a more marked effect of roll due to yaw (secondary effect of yaw/rudder) but that there is also an initial hesitation due to the inertia in roll.

You will notice that it accelerates considerably faster as soon as the nose is lowered.

High Speed Flight

From level cruise, set full power and you will notice a significant improvement in acceleration compared to the single. There will be the usual nose-up pitching moment due to the thrust and increasing airspeed but there will be little or no yaw.

Steep Turns and Spirals

The danger with the twin is that it can accelerate to V_{NO} and beyond very quickly when the nose is allowed to drop. Steep turns need to be flown with a firm control of attitude. Any tendency for the nose to drop should be immediately corrected—if necessary by momentarily reducing the bank angle.

Low Speed Flight

In level flight, close the throttles and allow the aircraft to decelerate while maintaining altitude. The twin is again similar to the single, with the nose down pitching moment due to the power reduction and also due to the reducing airspeed (increasing angle of attack). There is little or no yaw if the throttles are retarded simultaneously. Flying the aircraft at slow speed is not difficult and the aircraft will feel more stable than a small single. It will feel heavier/slower in roll.

Stalling

Stalling a twin is again similar to a single. If you close the throttles from straight and level flight, there will be a nose down pitching moment and the aircraft will decelerate. Raising the nose to maintain level flight will require increasing back pressure on the control column and there will be reduced airflow noise and reduced control power due to the reduced airflow and propeller slip stream. There is the pronounced nose-high attitude before the stall.

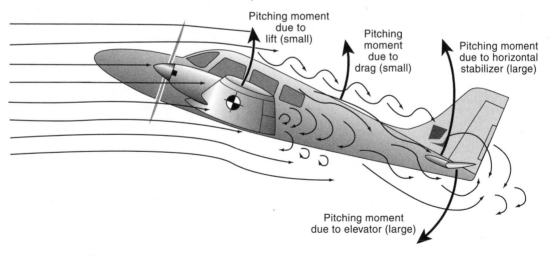

Pitching moment
due to
lift (small)

Pitching
moment
due to
drag (small)

Pitching moment
due to horizontal
stabilizer (large)

Pitching moment
due to elevator (large)

■ Pitching moments close to the stall

The control column will require a high pull-force (unless re-trimmed) and the displacement to the rear will be noticeable—in the pit of your stomach. Note this force and position. They are both valuable cues to an approaching stall. If ever you find you are pulling hard or the control column is a long way back (especially on base/final) watch out! You are about to lose it. You need to be extra careful at the point of stall to stop any yawing moment due to any slight asymmetry in thrust. Don't look at the balance ball. Look outside and keep straight by active use of the rudder.

The buffet prior to the stall will vary from aircraft to aircraft as will the stall warning horn. The stall itself is generally mild with the first indication being a rate of descent followed by a tendency for the nose to drop and perhaps some tendency for yaw or roll. Recovery is conventional by reducing the angle of attack but with care needed in power application to avoid too much asymmetry as the engines accelerate. The important thing as usual, is to stop any yaw. Looking *outside* is the way to detect it. Stalls with power on and with landing gear and flap down will vary according to the aircraft type and configuration (e.g. T-tail).

Cruise Descent

The most comfortable ride for passengers is provided by descending from an early enough point where you can maintain 500 ft per minute rate of descent until you reach the arrival point. If pressurized, remember to descend early enough to allow the *cabin* to descend and before descending, set pattern altitude at destination, plus 500 ft.

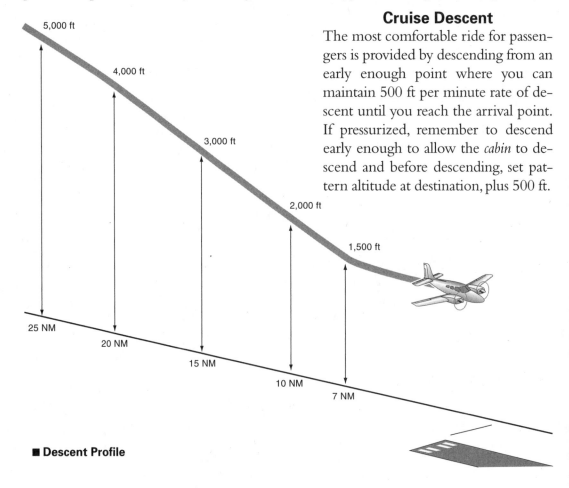

■ Descent Profile

You can plan to maintain V_{NO} in smooth air if you are in a hurry but watch the rate of descent. In case of any turbulence, reduce to V_A. A reasonable compromise is to set perhaps 20 kt below V_{NO} as a normal descent speed. In calm conditions, you can then increase to V_{NO} to increase rate of descent or distance travelled or if there is any turbulence, reduce to V_A. But check your Pilot's Operating Handbook. Remember V_A changes with weight. Anticipate turbulence due to thermals, cloud, or mechanical turbulence near hills. Slow down *beforehand*.

A recommended descent profile is calculated by using 5 × altitude = distance to go, i.e. from 7,000 ft start the descent at 35 NM and maintain cruise airspeed. The attitude and power will vary slightly from aircraft to aircraft but typical figures would be 18 in. (20 in. for turbochargers) and 2,400 RPM. The aircraft will reach 1,500 ft at about 8 miles still at cruise descent airspeed. This will typically be 140-180 kt. After levelling, the aircraft will slow to 120 kt (and gear speed) by 5 miles and be ready to enter the traffic pattern at a safe speed without further power adjustment.

Mixture, Turbos and Carburetor Heat

You have probably been taught to select full rich before descending in the training area or on navigation flights. If you have been cruising at higher altitudes at colder temperatures and for longer periods, you have to be cautious not to cool the engine too quickly—especially if it is turbocharged. Plan on 2 in. maximum MP reduction per 1,000 ft if you are descending at 500 fpm.

A general rule-of-thumb that is suggested by engine manufacturers is as follows:

If you have say 23 in. and 2,300 RPM for cruise, then select 21 in. and leave the mixture lean and the cowl flaps closed. As you descend, the manifold pressure will tend to increase. Maintain the 21 in. If you have been in economical cruise at perhaps 20 in., then leave that set and reduce the RPM to 2,000 for the initial descent and maintain the 20 in. as you descend. Leave the mixture set as it was until you are about to level off and increase to cruise power at the lower altitude.

If appropriate, i.e. if there is any possibility, select carb heat to hot before reducing power for the descent and if visual, select cold before increasing power as you level. As a guide, don't make *any* large or sudden changes in power after prolonged cruising (no more than 2 in. MP at a time).

Visual Landing Pattern

It is a matter of professionalism to arrive in the pattern at the correct altitude, heading and speed. Joining the pattern is routine but allow extra time and distance to decelerate to V_{LO} (gear speed). Complete the pre-landing checks early so that you can concentrate on the pattern entry and other traffic. If you are used to flying a high-wing single, you will appreciate the much improved field-of-view when maneuvering in the pattern.

Approach and Normal Landing

The pattern itself is normal but allow a little further lateral displacement on downwind than your little single. Establish the downwind spacing so that the wingtip is tracking down the centerline of the runway. Check the surface wind.

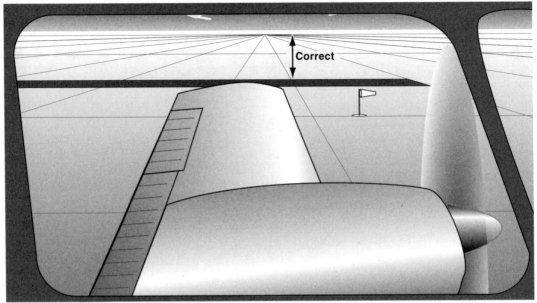

■ **Downwind spacing—left pattern**

The appearance on a right hand downwind is very different for the same spacing.

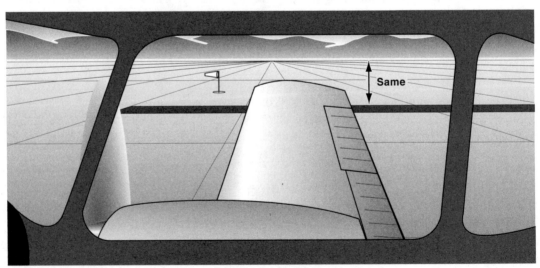

■ **Downwind spacing—right pattern**

Complete the pre-landing checks early. With a retractable landing gear select down and then wait for three greens. Don't continue the pre-landing checks until you have 3 greens. It is usual to lower partial flap (the first stage), abeam the touchdown point, before reaching base.

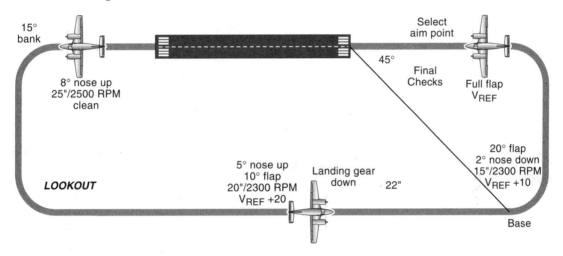

■ Diagram of pattern—Bushcraft 71

It is important to set attitudes and power around the pattern. If you do, the accuracy of your flying will improve and at the same time, the workload will be low.

Ask your instructor for the attitudes and power settings to be used in the pattern. Remember, *power + configuration + attitude = performance*, and if you set them accurately, the aircraft will fly itself and you can concentrate on the pattern, wind, traffic and checklist.

The Captain of the B747 Jumbo sets attitude (+7.5°), thrust (EPR 1.18), configuration (Flaps 5) and this stabilizes the aircraft on downwind at V_{REF} + 40. It's as simple as that and it works for our little aircraft just as effectively.

We have made a reference table for our Bushcraft 71. It is most useful.

Flightpath	Attitude	Power	Performance
Climb	+8°	25"/2,500 RPM	1,100 fpm 100 KIAS
Fast cruise	+3°	25"/2,500 RPM	Level 145 KIAS
Slow cruise	+5°	23"/2,300 RPM	Level 130 KIAS
Cruise descent	–3°	20"/2,300 RPM	500 fpm 130 KIAS
Approach	–2° Full flap	14"/Full Fine	400 fpm 78 KIAS 3° G/S

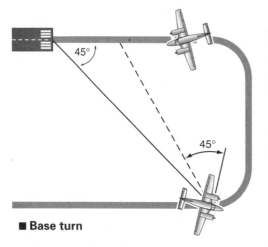

■ Base turn

Start the stopwatch abeam the threshold and start the base turn at +30 seconds (no wind) ±5 seconds per 10 kt of headwind or tailwind at pattern altitude. (The timing is a very useful guide for night and limited visibility approaches as will be discussed later).

Alternatively, use a visual base turn position 45° from the runway centerline, measured from the threshold (45° from the threshold centerline *not* the aircraft—as you may have drift correction applied.) Reduce the power to the recommended setting, holding the attitude level as you enter the turn (so the airspeed settles). Select the next stage of flap and as the airspeed reaches the approach value, adjust the attitude for the descending turn.

Don't allow the airspeed to come below Blue Line until you are ready to lower full flap on final, are committed to land and are certain to reach the threshold. Turn through the base leg heading to allow for wind and set the straight descent attitude. Trim. Assess the glideslope and expected headwind on final and adjust the power and flap if required.

Monitor the centerline and turn early rather than late—especially if you have any tailwind component on base. Remember to trim the aircraft when the attitude is set. Imagine the centerline extended and scan from the far end of the runway to the threshold. This gives a good line reference for your roll-out. Anticipate the effect of wind on the final turn.

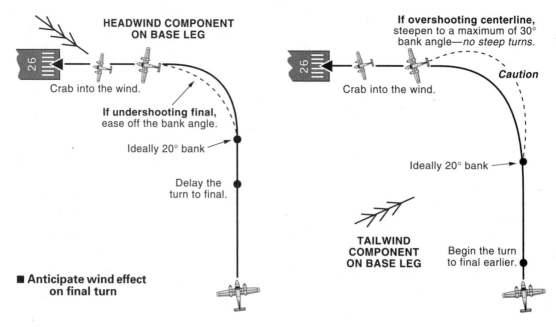

■ Anticipate wind effect on final turn

Adjust the bank in the final turn but at the same time, be conscious of the pitch attitude. It is very easy to allow the nose to drop during the base to final turn.

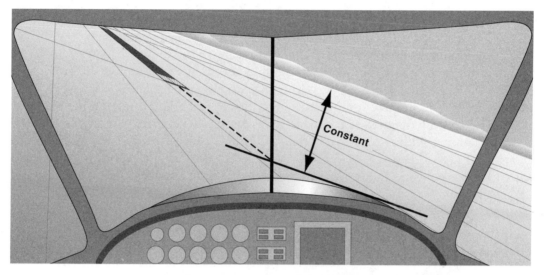

■ **Maintain attitude in the final turn**

Your initial view of the runway as you roll out on final, entirely determines the glidepath you are to follow. Now is the time to correct it. Also if your power adjustment on base was insufficient or over generous, this is the last chance for a significant correction. Until now you will have been aiming generally for the threshold.

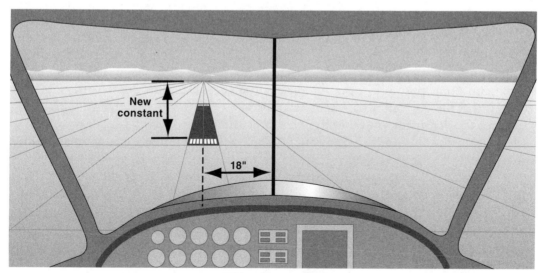

■ **Lined-up on final**

If you have captured a 3° glideslope (±½°), set the prop levers to full-fine (max RPM) and confirm the landing gear lights. Adjust the attitude and power and trim the aircraft. Avoid the tendency to allow too much lateral displacement for your offset seating. Your eyes are only 18 inches from the longitudinal axis of the aircraft so line up so that your eyes are aligned with the centerline (to be precise 18 in. left of centerline).

(It is interesting to stand behind the left-hand seat in a full flight simulator, check that the left hand pilot is lined-up on the centerline and then stand behind the right hand seat. You will see that the right hand pilot is also on the centerline!)

Now decide whether to commit yourself to the approach. You can continue but delay full flap and speed reduction. If you have a clearance to land, if the runway is clear and if you are content with the approach, then continue. If not, delay full flap and don't let the airspeed reduce below V_{YSE}. When *certain*, select full flap, props full fine, mixtures rich, carb heats cold and then re-trim. Complete the final checks (props, undercarriage, flaps, clearance). Now come back to V_{REF}.

Aim Points

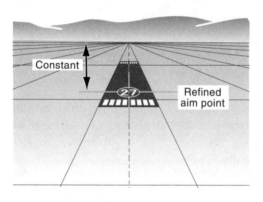

Constant

Refined aim point

■ **Adjusting the aim point**

What is the aim point? The aim point is where your eyes would impact the runway if you didn't flare. You should now be aiming for the numbers on the runway beyond the piano keys or even the 1,000 ft marker if you are using a longer runway with VASI or PAPI. Refine the aim point and make small continuous corrections to fly your eyes to impact the aim point. The attitude and heading may be varying and the aim point will not necessarily be in a constant position in the windscreen. (Only when established in a constant configuration, at a constant speed, on a constant path and in calm condition will the aim point position in the windscreen be constant). This doesn't matter. What matters is that the corrections are achieving a constant *flightpath* to the aim point.

Control the flightpath with the flight controls and the airspeed with the throttles.

Monitor airspeed, attitude and aim point. There will be a tendency to over-adjust the power to correct airspeed changes. If you monitor the airspeed *trend* and *rate of change* as well as the actual reading and make small but early changes, then the accuracy will improve. Similarly, with attitude. As soon as you detect a vertical or lateral deviation in the flightpath, i.e. movement and trends of the aim point, make some immediate adjustment rather than waiting for it to develop.

Make lateral adjustment with aileron, coordinated with rudder. The rudder input significantly improves the directional response at low airspeed—i.e. it is easier and quicker to point the aircraft where you want it to go.

There are several reasons not to close the throttle before the flare. Closing the throttle causes:
- a *loss of lift* due to loss of slipstream;
- a *nose-down* pitching moment;
- a *loss* of slipstream and therefore download from the tailplane (this will cause a further nose–down moment)
- *reduced* elevator power due to loss of slipstream; and
- a *loss* of thrust.

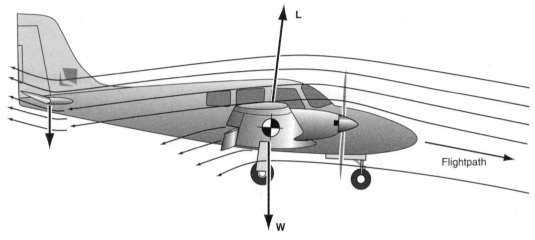

■ **Balance of forces on short final**

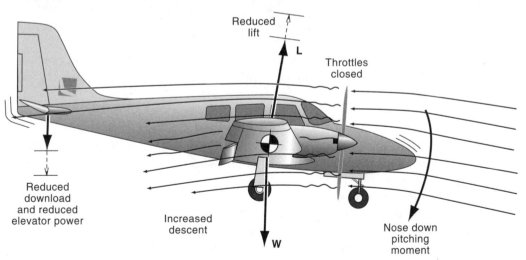

■ **Imbalance due to throttle closure**

All of these factors occur together and they are everything you don't want. You want to:
- *maintain* V_{REF} and carry the aircraft through the flares, which requires some thrust;
- *reduce* the rate of descent which requires some thrust; and
- *raise* the nose attitude and flightpath, which requires elevator power (i.e. airflow).

If you are concerned about excessive float in your aircraft by all means remove the thrust quickly but not *before* commencing the flare.

As you reach the flare point, progressively change your attention to the *center of the far end of the runway* and progressively change the attitude of the aircraft so that the flightpath will now carry you to that point.

As the change of flightpath changes, reduce the power and actively hold the attitude as you do so. Keep straight with rudder and maintain the wings level—unless some drift starts to develop (in which case, lower the into-wind wing slightly). The aircraft will touch down by itself. Hold the attitude on touchdown and lower the nose gently under control. (Airline training captains refer to a second "flare" for the nosewheel.) When the nosewheel is on the ground, commence braking. Apply the brakes for a few seconds then release the pressure then reapply. It is important to reduce speed early to below 30 kt or so. Delaying the braking lengthens the ground roll significantly.

Touch-and-Go Landing

For a touch-and-go you should identify and select the flap to the *takeoff* or *up* setting and reapply power. Be careful when retracting the flap as it is possible in some aircraft to inadvertently select the *landing gear*. You may need to re-trim. Be careful not to be looking inside the cockpit for too long. Try to feel and reach the controls and only look as a quick check. For re-trimming it is valuable to practice and to remember how long for electric trim or how much wheel movement to approximately reset the trim from landing to takeoff.

Reintroduce full power and be careful to balance the power levers and to keep straight as you do so. Continue for a normal takeoff and be ready for an engine failure.

Short-Field Landing

It could be argued that for a twin, there is no such thing as a short-field landing. Runway length is required to meet certain requirements and therefore a normal approach is acceptable—and preferred.

A short-field landing is one where landing distance available is marginal, but acceptable, where you perhaps wish to stop short of patches of water or gravel or to turn off early to allow following traffic to land.

The pattern is normal. The approach is normal. The approach angle is normal. However, the aim point is critical. To be precise with an approach, a pilot needs to know what he's aiming for or at.

For a normal approach we want to cross the threshold at a height which does not expose us to a risk of undershooting and which gives a touchdown with room to stop within the available length of the runway.

For a short-field landing you have to:
- accept an increased risk of undershooting by using an aim point at or close to the threshold; and
- minimize the *float* and ground roll.

However, reducing the approach angle increases the risk of undershooting and exposes the aircraft to downdrafts, obstacles and gusts and makes the approach more difficult to judge:
- the runway view is non-standard;
- the nose attitude is higher;
- the power settings are higher; and
- terrain and obstacle clearance is reduced.

The better way to go is to retain the 3° path but adjust the aim point. The other parameter that we can control, and which directly affects float and ground roll, is threshold speed.

Once the approach is stabilized and if the conditions are suitable, it is acceptable to reduce the approach speed to say 1.15 times V_{SO} (but in this situation it is even more important to carry the power until after the flare begins, i.e. when the aircraft has responded and the flightpath has changed).

After the flare, the throttles can be quickly closed, the braking commenced and the control column held back to protect the nosewheel and propellers.

Crosswind Landing

Because of the greater span and the higher inertia in roll, use the crab technique on final and through the flare. In the flare, lower the into-wind wing to prevent drift. (This is known as the *combination technique*.)

Don't adjust the V_{REF} for windspeed but for *gust factor*. As a general rule add half the gust factor to V_{REF}, i.e. if the wind is 20 kt gusting to 30 then add ½ of 10 = 5 kt to your V_{REF}. Discuss this with your instructor.

Shutdown and Post-flight Inspection

Before shutdown, run the engines at fast idle for at least a minute to stabilize the temperatures—especially the turbos.

It is valuable practice to carry out a post-flight inspection especially for stone or bird damage and for leaks (fuel, oil, struts on brakes). They can be fixed before they become a problem for the next flight.

Performance Table For Your Aircraft

Flightpath	Attitude	Power	Performance
Climb			
Fast cruise			
Slow cruise			
Cruise descent			
Approach			

The above data card with the data for your aircraft would be a most useful reference to add to your kneeboard.

Chapter 4

Understanding Asymmetrics

Forces and Moments

Before discussing the factors affecting an aircraft in asymmetric flight, let's make sure we are all on the same wavelength with regard to terminology.

Force

A force is simply a push or pull and it causes an acceleration in the direction in which it acts. In the case of an aircraft, the forces we are used to discussing are lift, weight, thrust and drag. As well as the linear effect of the force, if it does not act through the center of gravity, there is also a tendency to rotate the aircraft about one of its axes.

Axes and Motions

Remember there are three axes that are used to describe the motion of the aircraft:

- Pitching is the rotary motion about the lateral axis.
- Rolling is the rotary motion about the longitudinal axis.
- Yawing is the rotary motion about the vertical axis. Remember that this axis is vertical to the plane of the aircraft and not to the horizon.

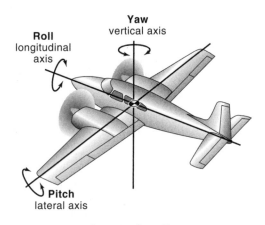

■ Axes and motions

Moments

The twisting force that is causing the rotary motion is called a *moment* and the distance between the line of action of the force and the pivot point or fulcrum is called the *moment arm*. The moment (the power of the twisting force) is the force multiplied by the moment arm. Obviously the longer the moment arm, the more leverage and therefore the more twist that is exerted.

Complex Forces and Moments

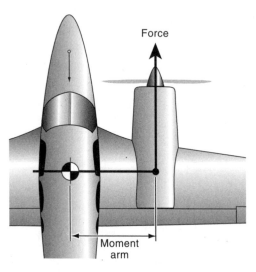

We describe the force or moment by what is causing it. In some cases, the moment is due to the secondary effect of another force or motion. In describing what is happening to an asymmetric aircraft, there are many to be taken into account.

■ **Moment arm**

Pitching Moments

- Pitching moment due to thrust.
- Pitching moment due to drag.
- Pitching moment due to the horizontal stabilizer.
- Pitching moment due to elevators or trim.
- Pitching moment due to lift.

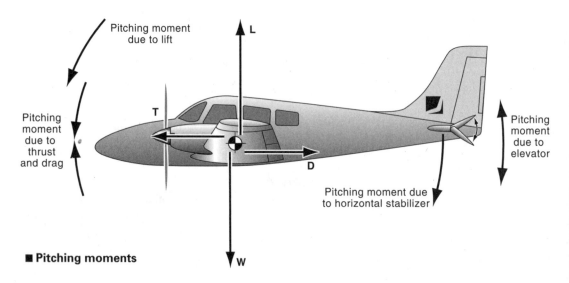

■ **Pitching moments**

Rolling Moments

- Rolling moment due to sideslip (uneven lift).
- Rolling moment due to yaw.
- Rolling moment due to aileron.
- Rolling moment due to rudder.

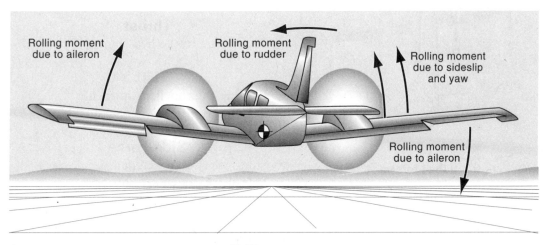

■ **Rolling moments**

Yawing Moments

- Yawing moment due to sideslip.
- Yawing moment due to rudder.
- Yawing moment due to aileron deflection.

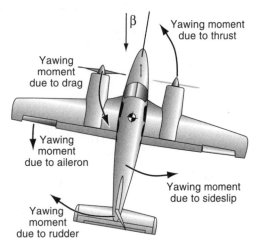

■ **Yawing moments**

51

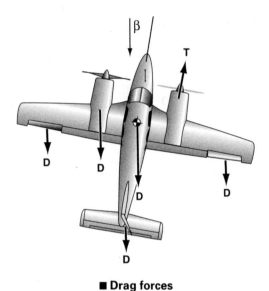

Drag forces

Drag

- Drag due to sideslip (frontal area).
- Drag due to the failed engine and wind-milling propeller, or
- Drag due to the feathered propeller.
- Drag due to control surface deflections.

Thrust

- Thrust due to the live engine.

Lift

- Lift due to propeller slipstream.
- Lift due to sideslip.

Side-Force

- Side-force due to rudder.
- Side-force due to sideslip.
- Side-force due to bank.

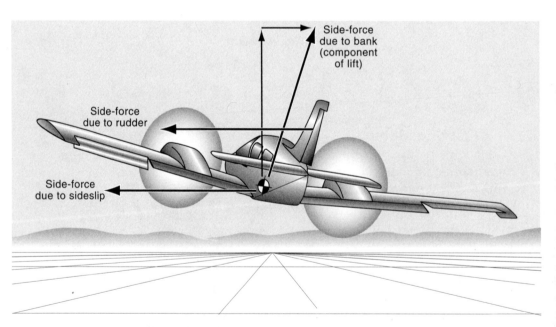

Side-forces in asymmetric flight

It's not complicated really. However, before we look more closely, let's redefine yaw, sideslip and balance.

Yaw, Sideslip and Balance

Yaw

Yaw is a rotary *motion* about the vertical axis. It stops as soon as the aircraft stops. There could still be a yawing moment but it must be countered by another otherwise the aircraft would continue to yaw.

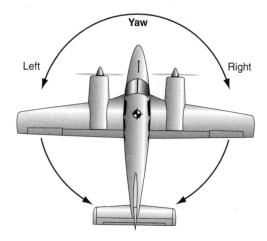

■ **Yawing motion**

Sideslip

Sideslip or sideslip angle is merely the sideways angle of attack.

You will be familiar with *alpha* for angle of attack (AOA). Sideslip is called *beta* (β).

It is the lateral component of the angle between the longitudinal axis of the aircraft and the relative airflow.

It is important to note this characteristic to be able to understand what is happening to the aircraft.

Unfortunately we don't have a sideslip indicator (nor an angle of attack indicator—the two most important pieces of information to a pilot—but that's another story).

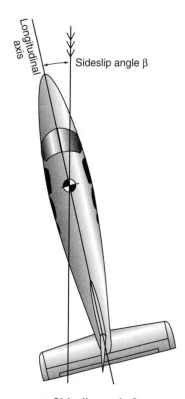

■ **Sideslip angle β**

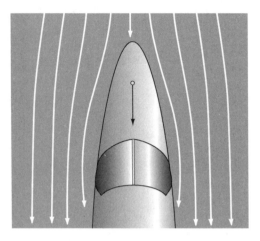

■ Yaw string

We can make do without the sideslip indicator but to understand what is happening when an engine fails, we will attach a piece of wool to the upper surface of the nose and use this as a crude but effective sideslip indicator. Glider pilots use this device to obtain maximum aerodynamic efficiency— (minimum drag).

Balance

Balance as measured by the balance ball or skid ball is another matter.

Imagine you are riding a Harley and you suspend a rock on the end of a piece of string. As you accelerate, the rock will hesitate and cause the string to tilt. When you are stabilized at cruise speed, the rock will return to a vertical position under the influence of gravity. (In practice, it will hang back a little due to aerodynamic drag.)

■ Pendulum effect—accelerating

■ Steady speed

When you turn, say to the right, the stone will initially be left behind and will sway to the left of the vertical axis of the Harley and then as the turn stabilizes, it will return to the central position—relative to the Harley. It is balanced under the influence of gravity (W), and centrifugal reaction (CR).

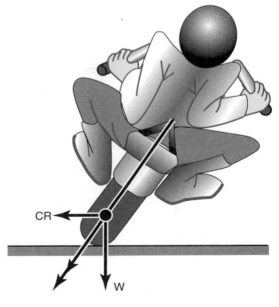

■ Balance in the turn

■ **Unbalanced**

If you lean over and do not turn, the stone will stay vertical under the influence of gravity—and you will fall over. There is no centripetal force and therefore no centrifugal reaction.

■ **Balance Ball**

The balance ball is the stone. It shows the force of gravity unless affected by other forces or accelerations. In which case, it shows the resultant of gravity and the other forces. In a balanced turn, it shows the resultant of gravity and the centrifugal reaction to the turn—just like the stone.

If you bank the aircraft and stop the yaw due to sideslip with opposite rudder (*top* rudder), then the ball will hang down on the inside of the bank under the influence of gravity. The aircraft is not balanced but nor is it accelerating.

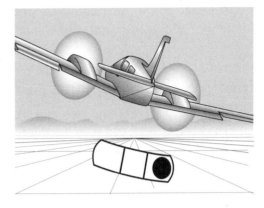

■ **Banked but unbalanced**

If you yaw the aircraft with rudder and stop the roll due to yaw with opposite aileron, i.e. keep the wings level, the ball will move opposite to the applied rudder. As the aircraft yaws and sideslips, the ball is left behind.

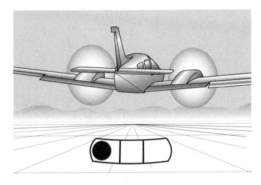

■ **Level but unbalanced**

To summarize the various indications let's compare the following:

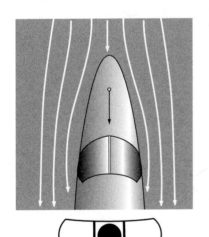

■ **Straight flight**

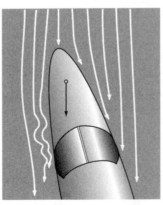

■ **Sideslip**

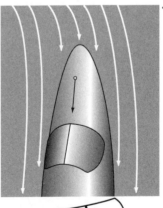

■ **Balanced turn**

The left aircraft is in balanced straight and level flight, the center aircraft is in a steady sideslip (wings level), and the right aircraft in a balanced left hand turn.

The Forces and Moments at Work

In symmetrical level flight at a constant airspeed, the flightpath is straight, level and stabilized. If the aircraft is in trim, the forces and moments are balanced.

Normal Flight

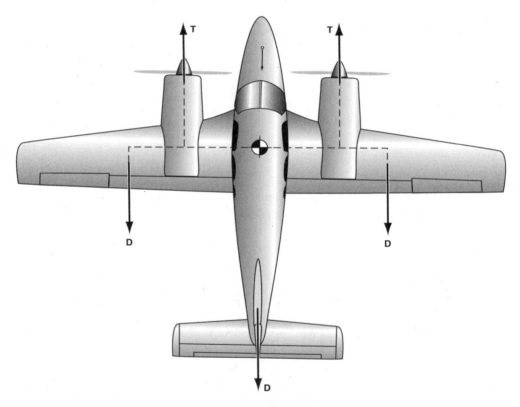

■ Forces and moments are balanced

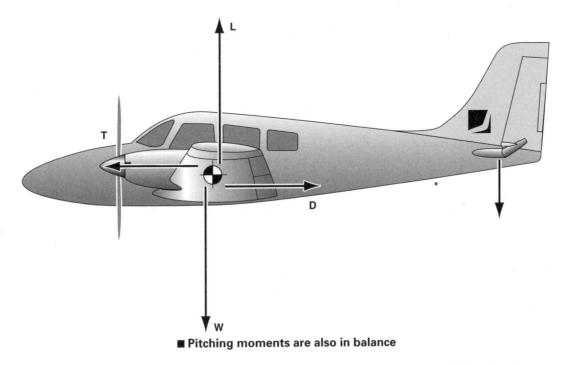

■ Pitching moments are also in balance

The pitching moments are balanced by the horizontal stabilizer and elevator trim.

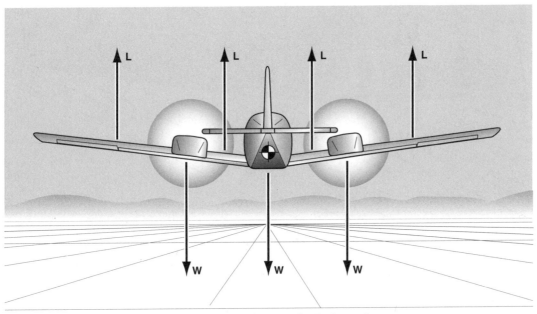

■ Rolling moments—also balanced

There are no significant rolling or yawing moments in balanced flight other than small fuel imbalances or minor variations in thrust from each engine. The twin has rudder trim and in many cases, aileron trim, to balance these small moments.

Engine Failure

Now let's consider the case of engine failure. When an engine fails there is an immediate reduction of thrust and an increase in drag on the side of the failed engine. This affects the balance between total thrust and total drag and therefore the aircraft will immediately decelerate.

The loss of thrust causes the nose to drop and the airspeed to decay. The loss in total lift and the reducing airspeed will cause the aircraft to descend. The descending flight-path plus loss of slipstream over the horizontal stabilizer in most twins causes a nosedown pitching moment.

■ **Nose-down pitching moment**

The difference in thrust and drag causes an immediate yawing moment towards the dead engine. The yaw causes an immediate sideslip and the fin and keel surfaces battle to keep the aircraft pointing into the relative airflow. At high airspeed, this stabilizing force is powerful. At low airspeed, it is overwhelmed by the yaw due to asymmetric thrust.

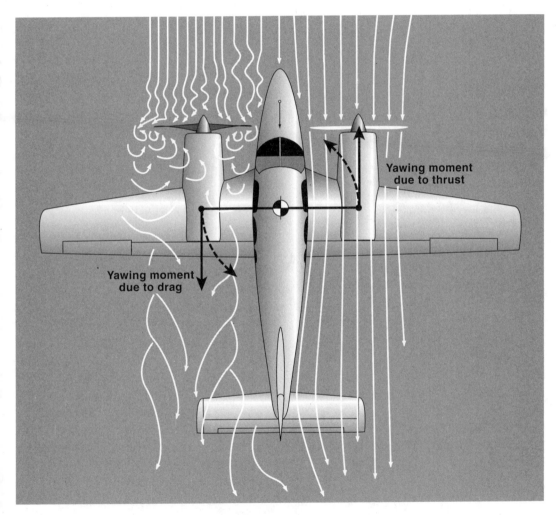

Yawing moment due to thrust

Yawing moment due to drag

■ Instant of failure

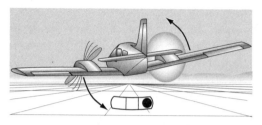

■ **Roll due to yaw, lift and sideslip**

There is an immediate reduction in lift on the side of the failed engine due to the reduced slipstream and thus there is a rolling moment towards the dead engine.

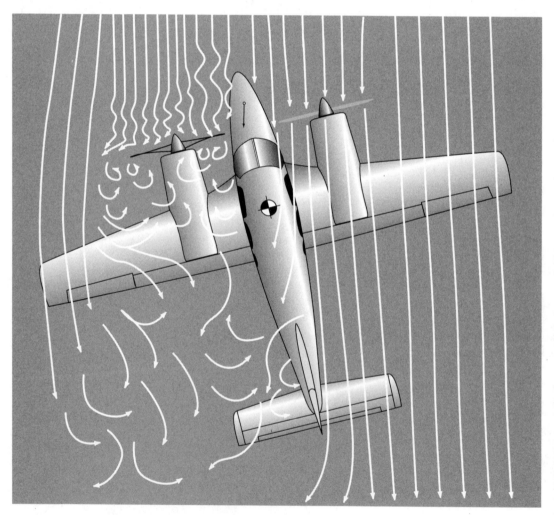

■ **Yaw and loss of lift**

As the yaw rate develops, the roll due to yaw combined with the roll due to sideslip now causes a pronounced roll towards the failed engine.

The aircraft descends more rapidly now. It enters what is effectively a steepening spiral dive with the asymmetric thrust, drag and lift overcoming the natural stability.

It will not recover unaided.

Flight Sequence—Uncorrected Engine Failure

Thus at the instant of failure, the aircraft wants to yaw and roll towards the dead engine, and to decelerate and descend. If the pilot did nothing, this is exactly what the aircraft would do.

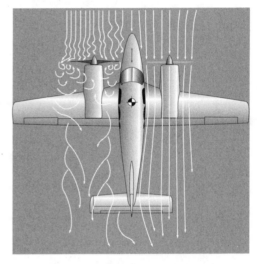

■ **Drag, yaw, loss of performance**

But worse: If the aircraft is allowed to yaw, the rolling moment due to yaw causes further roll and sideslip. The aircraft will quickly enter a steepening, descending spiral. Typically it yaws, rolls, hesitates, yaws, rolls, departs.

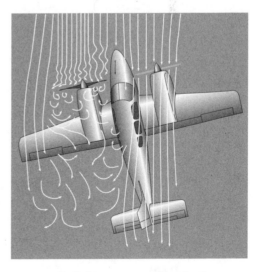

■ **Roll due to yaw and sideslip**

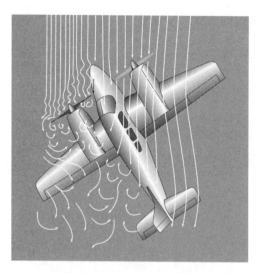

■ **Nose dropping, further roll**

The nose will continue to drop and the airspeed will start to increase due to the steepening descent path.

It is this latter stage, when the yaw rate is allowed to develop and to induce further rolling moments, which can lead to loss of control.

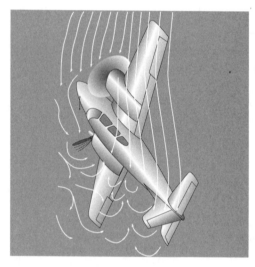

■ **Yaw, roll and pitch**

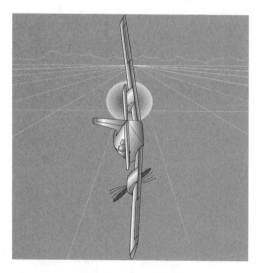

■ **Loss of control**

Control can now only be regained by closing the throttle of the live engine and recovering from the dive—altitude permitting.

In relation to engine failure, two aspects are significant:

• control; and
• performance.

Firstly we must restore control.

Control After Engine Failure

The pilot's immediate and most vital task on engine failure is to *STOP THE YAW.*

If you can't stop the yaw with full rudder then you can only control the aircraft by reducing thrust on the live engine. Either way it must be stopped—even if you have to accept a severe performance loss as a result. It is the *only* way to regain control.

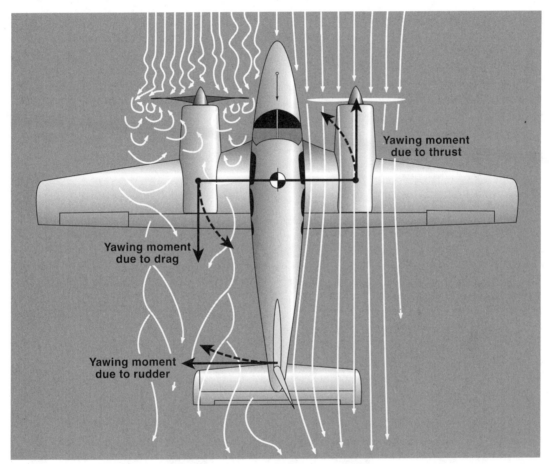

■ **Rudder to stop the yaw developing**

We will discuss some refinements and other influences in a moment, but always remember the importance of this first action. In some aircraft, the roll due to yaw is so pronounced that the pilot perceives the roll and sideslip before any noticeable yaw rate develops. That is, there is some yaw and then a slight hesitation as the sideslip and keel surfaces fight to keep the aircraft straight. Then there is roll due to sideslip and further yaw. If you allow time for the pilot to react it is easy to see how they reacted instinctively to the roll rather than the yaw.

Many have died as a result of trying to stop the roll with aileron before applying the opposite rudder. The deflected aileron added to the drag and to the yaw. Because the roll due to yaw was so powerful, these pilots could only have regained control if they had first stopped the yaw. Sounds a little dramatic! It is. Let's assume the pilot has reacted correctly and stopped the yaw and then the roll. What next?

Refinements/Finesse

We are looking for control with the least loss of performance.

Control is possible in three ways:

• bank towards the live engine with no rudder;
• use rudder to stop yaw, wings level; and
• use rudder to stop yaw, slight bank.

We will consider the pros and cons of all three but the first option is not viable in practice since it is too dangerous and offers the greatest loss of performance.

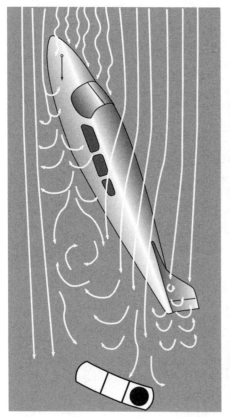 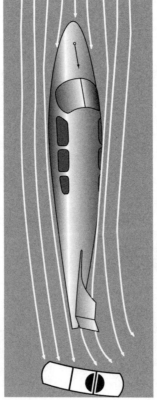 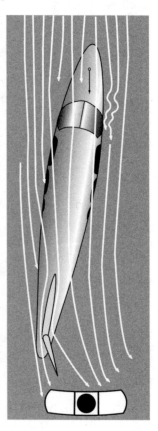

■ **Bank only (massive drag)**   ■ **rudder plus bank (least drag)**   ■ **rudder only (wings level)**

Option One

Bank Towards the Live Engine—No Rudder

We can allow the directional stability to stop the yaw (and it would at certain airspeeds), but we would have to stop the roll and the aircraft would be flying sideways. Drag is enormous due to the increased frontal area that is presented to the relative airflow and due to the need for a higher angle of attack to compensate for the reduced vertical component of lift (because of the bank angle).

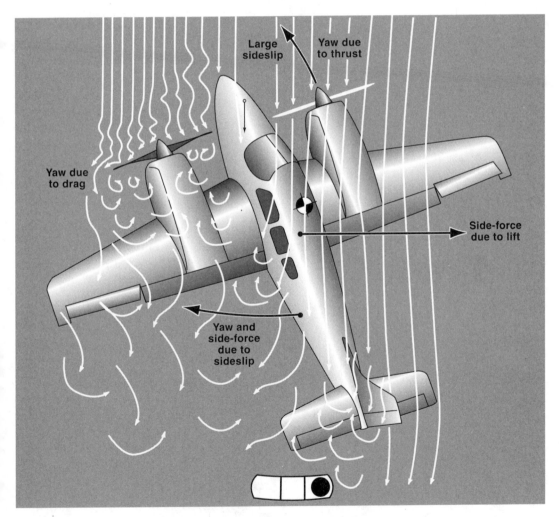

■ Allowing sideslip to stop the yaw

Note the dreadful imbalance. The aircraft has a very high angle of sideslip, a relatively high angle of bank, grossly increased frontal area (and consequent drag), large aileron deflection and a large *blanketed* area of the wing (and loss of lift). This aircraft is going nowhere.

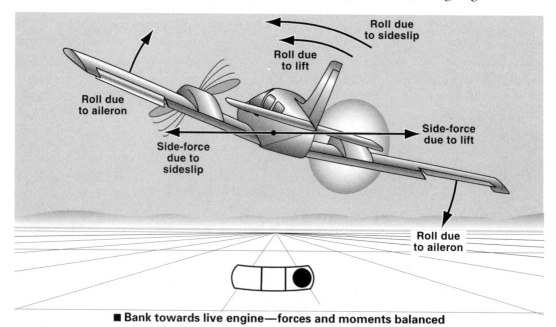

■ **Bank towards live engine—forces and moments balanced**

There is also a risk of fin stall or structural damage. The fin is an airfoil and at 16° of sideslip, it will stall, just like a wing. If this happens, there isn't enough directional stability to stop the yaw. Control will be lost. Also consider if the sideslip is allowed to develop and *then* full rudder is applied—immediate fin stall!

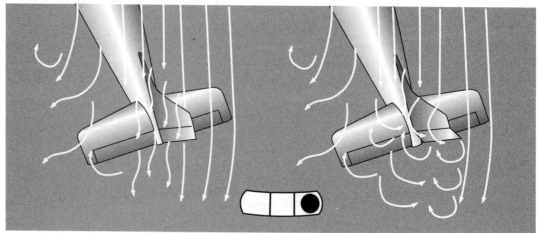

■ **Fin stall due to rudder deflection**

Option Two

Rudder to Stop Yaw—Wings Level

We can use rudder to prevent yaw and we can maintain the wings level with aileron. This is called the *wings-level* method. This method works but we are not making best use of our control power as the rudder is having to fight against the directional stability. However, the technique does have some other advantages. It is easy to fly because the wings are level and the skid ball is centered.

There is some extra drag due to sideslip and therefore reduced performance. The technique can be used for control in the cruise but it does not offer the absolute best performance for critical situations such as engine failure after takeoff.

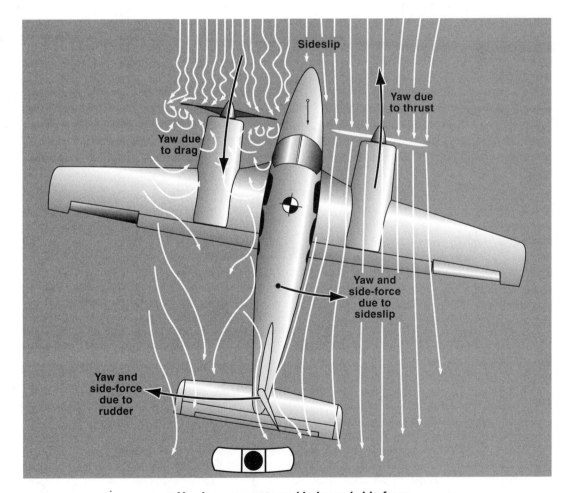

Sideslip

Yaw due to thrust

Yaw due to drag

Yaw and side-force due to sideslip

Yaw and side-force due to rudder

■ **Yawing moments and balanced side-force**

This method is a compromise between orientation and performance. It does not offer the least drag and therefore not the maximum potential performance that can be achieved with the third option, as we will see.

However, the relatively small performance loss is exchanged for powerful visual references, external and internal to ensure that the body's sensations can be orientated. Not only are the wings level (horizon and attitude indicator), but the balance ball and turn indicator are also centered.

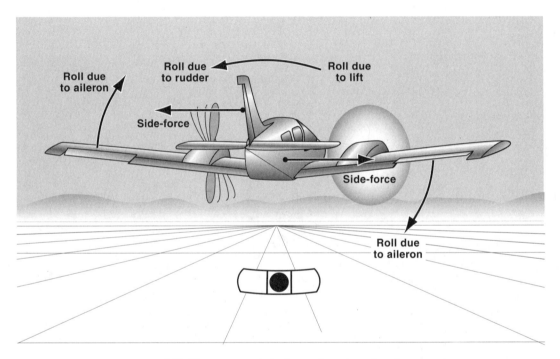

■ Rolling moments balanced—wings level

In a turn or in IMC and during the approach, especially in crosswind conditions, having the balance ball centered or wings level provides a useful reference, and for this reason, many instructors recommend the wings-level method for all situations except engine failure on takeoff. Further, the human body can get very confused between bank, balance, sideslip and yaw and can actually become so confused that it is not sure which engine has failed! If in doubt center the ball with rudder and work it out from there.

Option Three

Rudder to Stop Yaw, Slight Bank Towards Live Engine

With rudder against yaw, and slight bank towards the live engine there is zero sideslip. This is the most efficient way to control the aircraft, to make best use of available control, to minimize drag and to gain the most performance that is available. Part of the lift vector is used to balance the side-force due to rudder and thus allows the sideslip to be reduced to zero. Zero sideslip results in minimum drag. It is called the *angle of bank* method and offers the best performance. The maximum recommended bank is 5°.

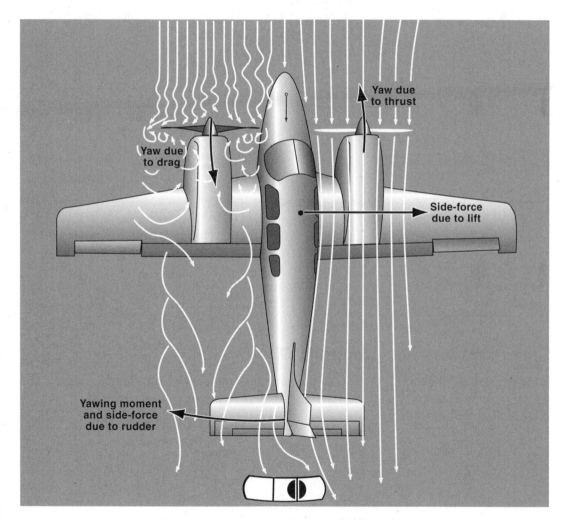

■ **Yawing moments and balanced side-force**

Note that the aircraft has 3-5° of bank towards the live engine and the balance ball is displaced slightly. This can become a vague reference in IMC or in turbulence. If ever in doubt, level the wings with aileron and center the ball with rudder. Then reapply bank towards the live engine to restore best climb performance.

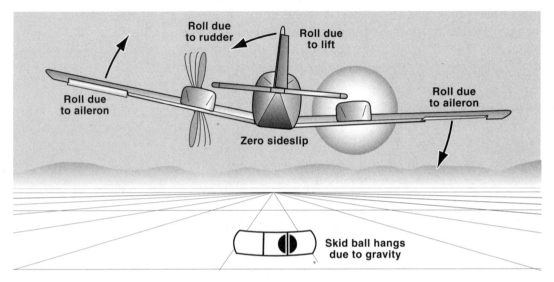

■ Rolling moments balanced

The skid ball is not centered but the aircraft is neither slipping nor skidding. This can be confirmed with our tuft of wool. In this instance, it is straight.

Having examined means of maintaining control, let's consider factors which can affect whether the aircraft is controllable at all.

Factors Which Affect Controllability

Factors which determine the degree of controllability are those which affect the yawing and rolling moments and the power of the flight controls to balance these moments. They are:
- thrust on the live engine;
- altitude;
- drag from the dead engine and propeller;
- P factor;
- torque reaction;
- difference in lift due to slipstream;
- CG position; and most important of all
- airspeed.

Thrust on the Live Engine

Obviously the greater the thrust, the greater the yawing moment from the live engine. Thrust is greatest at low speed.

Altitude

As thrust reduces with increasing altitude (allowing for the ability of turbochargers to maintain sea level thrust to a certain altitude), then, as a rule, the worst case for engine failure is at the lowest altitude, i.e. immediately after takeoff.

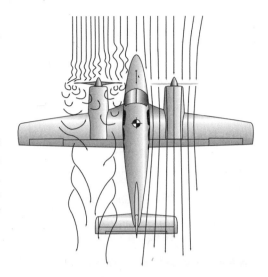

■ **Drag from windmilling propeller**

Drag from the Dead Engine

Drag from the dead engine contributes directly to the yawing moment and only the fact of whether the propeller is stopped, wind milling or feathered will alter the total drag and therefore the yawing moment from this engine.

There is, of course, a chance that the failure is partial and the propeller may be delivering some thrust but the measure of controllability is ultimately measured by whether the pilot can maintain directional control.

Drag from the windmilling propeller is high. The wind-milling propeller is working in reverse. It is being driven, i.e. it is reacting to the relative airflow and generating both lift and drag—components of the total reaction—just like any airfoil.

If we resolve this total reaction to components along the aircraft's flightpath (drag) and at right angles to the flightpath (lift or, in this case, torque to keep the propeller wind milling), then you can see the significant difference between this and a feathered propeller, which has not only reduced drag but

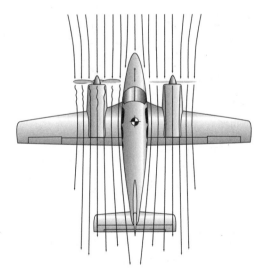

■ **Reduced drag from feathered propeller**

also no torque—which itself produces induced drag (sometimes called negative thrust.)

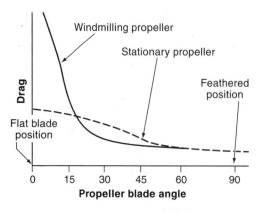

■ Propeller drag—windmilling versus feathered propeller

The drag from a windmilling propeller actually exceeds the drag from a stationary propeller, even if it is not feathered. At flat blade angles, the difference is very significant.

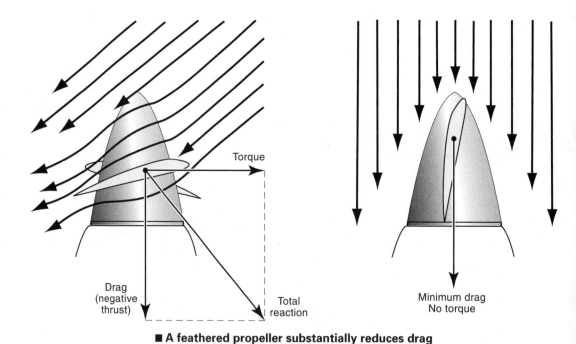

■ A feathered propeller substantially reduces drag

P Factor (Position of the Center of Thrust of the Live Engine)

There is a subtle difference in the yawing moment provided by each engine according to the direction of rotation of the propeller. At higher angles-of-attack of the aircraft and hence the axis of the engine, the down-going blade produces more thrust than the up-going blade because this blade is at a higher angle of attack to its relative airflow.

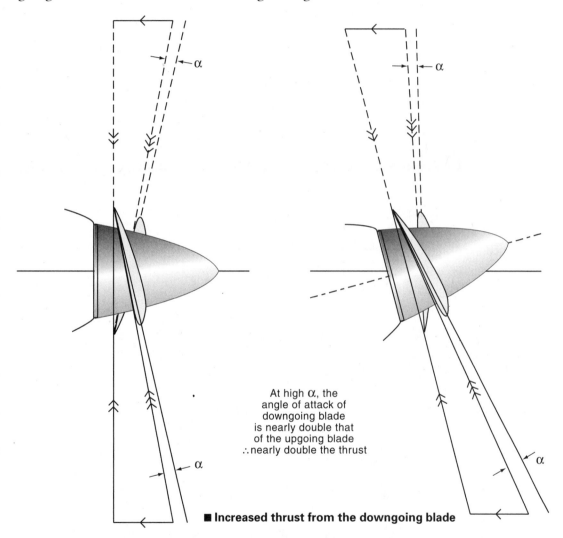

At high α, the angle of attack of downgoing blade is nearly double that of the upgoing blade ∴ nearly double the thrust

■ **Increased thrust from the downgoing blade**

This (P) factor determines the critical engine because at low airspeeds and therefore high angles-of-attack, the down-going blade causes the center of thrust to be displaced from the propeller shaft. If the engines rotate in the same direction, then it becomes evident that the worst case scenario is if the left engine fails as it leaves the engine with the longest moment arm (the distance of the thrust line from the CG) operating and this produces the greatest yawing moment (for engines which rotate in a clockwise direction when viewed from the cockpit).

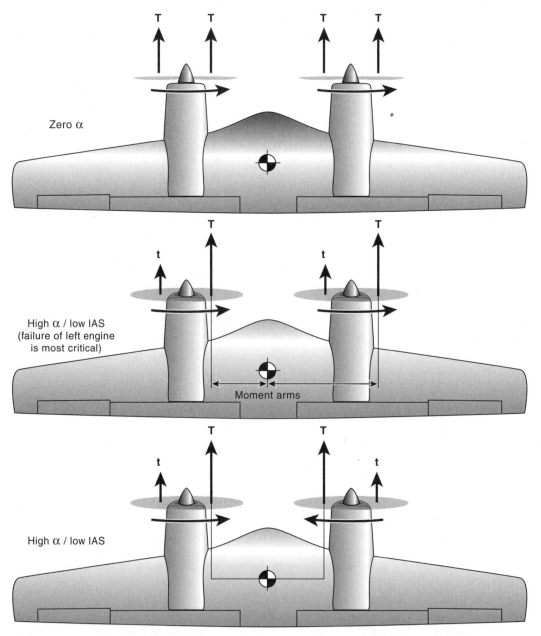

Zero α

High α / low IAS
(failure of left engine
is most critical)

Moment arms

High α / low IAS

■ **Eliminating critical engine by counter-rotation**

With counter-rotating engines there is no critical engine and also the direction of rotation is chosen to position the center of thrust inboard at high angles-of-attack. Not so important with 180 hp but in a WWII fighter such as a P38 or a Mosquito, with 1,500 hp per engine, it is attention-getting. *"Oh! Don't give me a P38, the props, they counter-rotate . . ."*

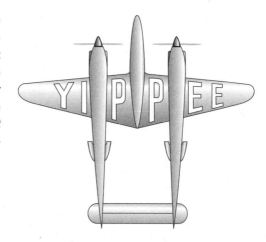

■ **Lockheed P38 Lightning**

Torque Reaction

To any applied force there is a reaction. When the engine turns the propeller, the reaction tries to turn the engine in the opposite direction. The tail tries to wag the dog. In a twin, the reaction is largely negated until one engine fails. Then the reaction is unbalanced. In the case of engines that rotate clockwise when viewed from the cockpit (standard for U.S. horizontally-opposed engines), then the torque reaction wants to roll the aircraft to the left. Failure of the left engine therefore is compounded as the torque reaction now adds to all of the other rolling moments.

Thus failure of the left engine is the more critical. With counter-rotating engines the right engine will now rotate counter-clockwise and the reaction will be to roll the aircraft to the right against the other forces and moments. Thus both P factor and torque reaction are minimized. There is no longer a critical engine.

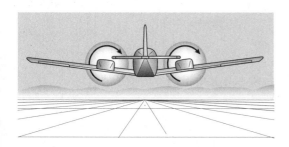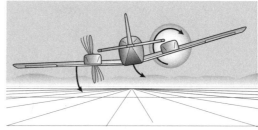

■ **Torque reaction—same-way engines—left engine fails**

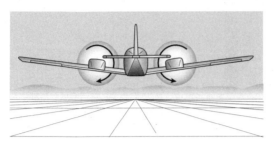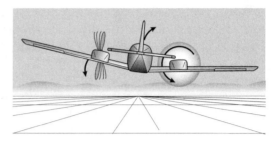

■ Torque reaction—counter rotating engines—left engine fails

So why do some twins have same engines? Lower cost of maintenance and commonality of spares—the tail wagging the dog again. Not much consolation when the left engine fails.

Difference in Lift

With engine failure on one side comes a loss in the propeller-induced lift on that side. As well as a reduction in the total lift and therefore a tendency to descend, there is a rolling moment towards the failed engine (yes, yet another one!) Feathering the propeller minimizes the distruption to the airflow.

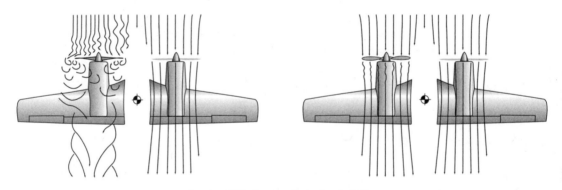

■ Loss of lift due to disturbed airflow

Position of the Center of Gravity (CG)

The CG position is important because it is the fulcrum about which the moments act. Moving it directly affects the length of the *tail moment arm,* that is the distance of the stabilizing moments from the balance point or center of rotation, and thus affects the leverage of the rudder and keel surfaces.

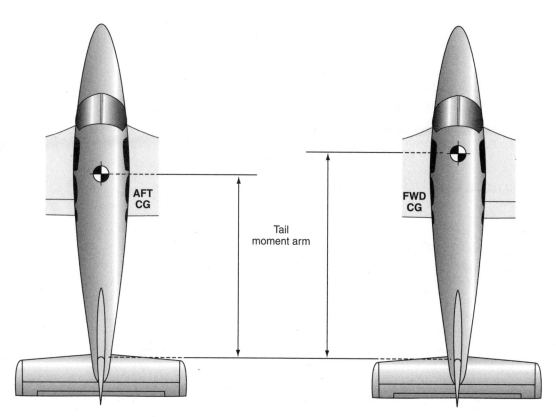

■ **Tail moment arm—fore and after CG position**

If the aircraft is loaded so that the CG is at its forward limit then the distance to the tail surfaces is at a maximum and the stabilizing moments are greatest, i.e. it is the most stable configuration. The rudder also has its greatest leverage. At the aft limit of CG position, the distance to the tail is minimized and so this offers the least stable position and the least rudder power.

Turbulence

Turbulence increases drag and demands control inputs which in turn further increase drag. Turbulence also makes control more difficult and more demanding. Accuracy is affected, and symptoms and cues are masked.

Airspeed

The aerodynamic power of all of the pilot's controls depends on indicated airspeed. More airspeed, more control power. Also, the stabilizing moments of the keel surfaces and the fin depend on indicated airspeed. More airspeed = more stability—both static and dynamic. Thrust reduces with increasing airspeed and altitude. Thus the yawing moment is reduced at higher airspeed. Drag from the failed engine also increases with airspeed but not significantly in comparison to the other elements. Overall, there is a significant improvement in controllability with increasing airspeed.

If things improve with increasing airspeed then conversely the situation deteriorates with reducing airspeed. Airspeed is the *vital* ingredient in controlling an aircraft with asymmetric thrust.

Minimum Control Airspeed

If airspeed is reduced with maximum thrust set on the live engine, a point is reached where full rudder deflection is required to prevent yaw. This condition is our minimum control speed, below which power on the live engine has to be reduced. Note there is no performance consideration—only control.

Minimum control speed will be demonstrated by your instructor and you will become familiar with the sensations and control forces.

The instructor is permitted to shut down an engine and feather the propeller above a specified minimum altitude. Below this, engine failure is simulated by closing the throttle and then setting zero thrust (which is equivalent to feathering the propeller).

Engine failure after takeoff can only be practiced in this way. You should let the tower controller know you will be practicing asymmetric patterns and simulated engine failure after takeoff (EFATO).

The school's operations manual or Standard Operating Procedures (SOPs) will specify the conditions for simulating engine failure.

The *minimum* speed for such practice is V_{SSE}.

V_{MC}

The minimum control speed relating to *sudden* engine failure on takeoff is a very specific speed measured under very stringent test conditions. It is known as V_{MC}.

Unlike the minimum control speed we have just discussed, V_{MC} is a dynamic case. It represents sudden and complete engine failure.

It is too dangerous to demonstrate or to practice, even at altitude. For training we use V_{SSE} (safe single engine speed), which gives a safety margin above actual V_{MC}. Under no circumstances should engine failure be simulated below V_{SSE}.

The specific factors for determination of V_{MC} by the test pilot, are as follows:
- Critical engine suddenly failed with the propeller in the fine pitch position and wind-milling. (Although there is an obvious improvement if the propeller is feathered and the speed could be further reduced, this case represents the real situation immediately following engine failure during takeoff.)
- Maximum thrust on the live engine.
- No more than 5° of bank towards the live engine.
- Landing gear retracted.
- Flaps in the takeoff position.
- CG at the aft limit for takeoff.
- Maximum takeoff weight.
- Sea level ISA (International Standard Atmosphere).
  There is no performance requirement—just control.

V_{MC} takes into account pilot skill, reaction time, strength (150 pounds force max) and assumes full rudder is available (seat position). The aircraft is allowed to deviate up to 20° in heading before the pilot regains control! Think about this. One hundred and fifty pounds force. This is more than many pilots weigh and it's not possible to put your full weight on the pedal. All you can do is push hard on the pedal against the resistance of the back of the seat. This is the main load bearing part of the structure—the seat, rail and back! You can't afford to have it fail or slide back. (Pilots who flew the Canberra bomber (B57 with manual controls) will recall the effort of wedging their shoulder against the ejection seat so that they could apply the required rudder force of nearly 300 lbs—but that's another story!)

Factors Affecting V_{MC}

There are many factors which influence V_{MC}.

Effect of Bank

Bank towards the live engine reduces the rudder deflection required and so allows a lower V_{MC}. But only a small amount of bank (less than 5°– typically 3°), because larger angles cause a significant reduction in the vertical component of lift and so require a higher angle of attack to maintain altitude. Consequently they incur more induced drag and there is a significant performance loss. The risks associated with greater bank angles and possible fin stall have already been highlighted.

Effect of CG Position

Because the CG is the point about which all moments act, the position of the CG directly affects the length of the tail moment arm and thus the power of the rudder and fin to maintain directional stability and control. Further, the destabilizing surfaces ahead of the CG are maximized at aft CG and minimized at forward CG. So, forward CG = greater control power and greater stability. Aft CG = reduced control power and reduced stability

Effect of Flap

Flap position affects total lift and drag, the nose down pitching moment and the stalling speed. Under asymmetric thrust conditions, the lowering of flaps reduces climb performance, increases the margin above the stall but does not directly affect V_{MC}. However, if takeoff flap is set, the difference in lift between the two wings due to the propeller slipstream is further increased. This increases the rolling moment, requires increased aileron deflection and indirectly affects V_{MC}.

Effect of Cowl Flaps

The cowl flaps directly increase drag but unlike flaps, they can be retracted individually. Thus we can leave the cowl flap on the live engine open for cooling and close the one on the failed engine. This reduces the drag on the dead side and the open one increases the drag on the live side. Both factors are favorable and would have a marginal effect on reducing V_{MC}.

Effect of Landing Gear

The landing gear symmetrically increases drag and thus directly affects performance but not control and so, does not affect V_{MC}. However the extended landing gear decreases directional stability because of the greater surface area ahead of the CG when the landing gear is extended. Thus the fin and rudder are opposed in sideslip conditions and this will slightly increase V_{MC}.

Effect of Altitude

V_{MC} is affected by maximum thrust which in turn reduces with increasing altitude. Therefore V_{MC} reduces with increasing altitude.

Relationship Between V_{MC} and V_{STALL}

The indicated airspeed at which the aircraft stalls is nominally constant for a given weight, in straight and level flight. If we are heavier or if we are turning, the stall speed increases but other than this, it doesn't vary with altitude. It is constant and therefore can be represented by a straight line on the graph.

The charts show that at about 3,000 ft, V_S and V_{MC} typically correspond. Note that the thrust of a normally aspirated engine reduces by the equivalent of 1 inch of manifold pressure for every thousand feet of altitude e.g. SL power of 29 in. reduces to 24 in. at 5,000 ft.

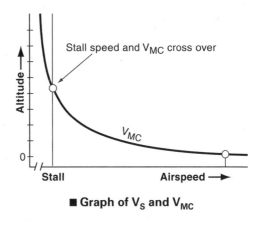

■ **Graph of V_S and V_{MC}**

So at a a certain altitude, the stalling speed is higher than V_{MC}. The significance of this, is that if we are slowing down with an engine failure and full power on the live engine, we may think we have a safe margin above V_{MC} and we have, but we could end up stalling with full power on one engine, almost full rudder deflection and the other engine wind-milling or feathered.

There isn't a more likely situation for an uncontrollable departure from controlled flight and if uncorrected, a spin.

Conclusion

Having examined V_{MC} in detail, it must now be said that it is a practically meaningless speed. We only need to know it so we can stay well away from it and to minimize our exposure—just like stalling speed. In many ways, the greatest risk with V_{MC}, as with V_S, is practicing it. The minimum speed at any time during practice should be V_{SSE} or if climb performance is a factor, V_{YSE}—Blue Line.

Performance After Engine Failure

Now that we have the aircraft under control we now have to cope with the performance loss. Airspeed is as vital to *performance* as it is to *control*.

Performance is determined by:
* thrust available vs. thrust required; and
* power available vs. power required.
Both of which depend on airspeed.

What Affects Performance?

Both thrust required and power required depend on drag. Obviously performance is adversely affected by anything that increases drag such as the propeller, landing gear, flap, cowl flaps, control deflections and turbulence. Having minimized these effects let's consider how to maximize residual performance after engine failure.

Performance depends on how much thrust or power is left after overcoming drag.

But, both thrust and power vary with airspeed—as does drag.

What Speed to Fly?—Power Versus Thrust

Remember *thrust* is how *hard* we can push whereas *power* determines how *fast* we can push. Thus *thrust* determines our instantaneous acceleration and angle of climb—but *power* determines our *speed, rate of climb* and *rate of fuel consumption*.

It's like comparing a tractor to a Ferrari. The tractor will pull the greatest load and climb the steepest incline (it has very high torque which is the same as thrust). However, the Ferrari will get to the top of the hill faster, i.e. in less time, and therefore has a greater rate of climb. The Ferrari gets to the top first (higher rate of climb) but the tractor climbs more steeply (higher gradient or angle of climb).

Can you imagine the Ferrari maintaining a 30° angle at 12 mph? Why not? Because its engine produces its greatest torque at high RPM and thus the car is performing best at high forward speed. You could of course give the Ferrari ridiculously low gearing. Similarly the tractor could be given higher gearing so that low speed and steep climb gradients are sacrificed for higher speed and rate of climb.

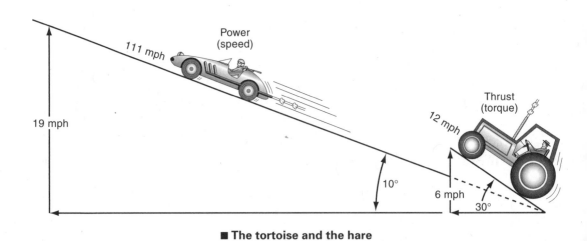

■ **The tortoise and the hare**

When we are considering aircraft performance whether on one or all engines, we need to consider whether the angle or the rate is the most important. At any particular speed in any particular configuration, the aircraft will be experiencing a certain amount of total drag. To maintain that speed, the engines have to produce a corresponding amount of thrust. If it is exactly equal then the speed won't change. If we wish to climb or accelerate from this point we must have some excess (spare) thrust available.

How much acceleration or how steep a climb is proportional to the amount of excess thrust at that speed. We are looking for the speed where the ratio of thrust to drag is greatest. Since thrust decreases with forward speed and total drag increases below and above minimum drag speed (V_{IMD}), then the best angle of climb is achieved at a speed below V_{IMD} but with a safe margin above the stall speed. The best airspeed for the maximum angle of climb is V_X or V_{XSE}.

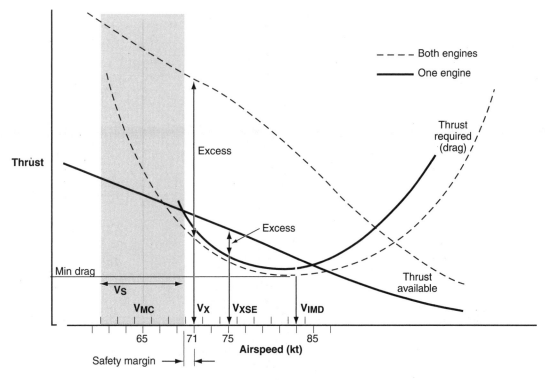

■ **Thrust available versus thrust required—Bushcraft 71**

The other measure of performance is *rate* of climb—how long it will take to reach pattern altitude. If we can get there quickly, then we can level off, reduce power, increase speed and improve controllability. We can then talk to someone and we can plan our recovery actions.

Time to climb depends on excess power. Power is the product of thrust and speed and although thrust reduces with forward speed, the total power available increases to a point because of the speed factor. Similarly, the power required is a measure of the total drag times the speed and so the excess (spare) power available, determines the available rate of climb and this occurs at a specific airspeed.

The airspeed for best rate of climb are V_Y and V_{YSE} as appropriate. They are above V_X and V_{XSE} and provide a safer margin. Unless there is a need to clear an obstacle, use V_Y or V_{YSE}.

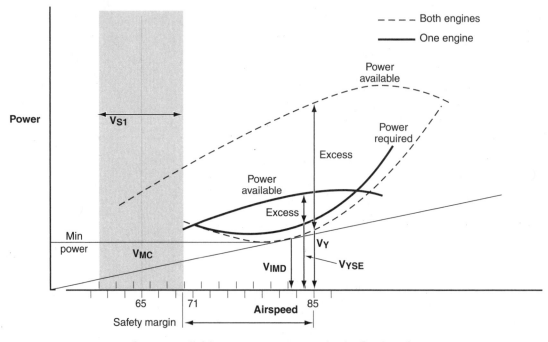

■ **Power available versus power required—Bushcraft 71**

Let's next look at the practical application of what we now know. Half thrust equals half climb performance? Not quite. Typically the light twin loses 80% of its excess (spare) thrust and hence 80% of its ability to climb or accelerate with engine failure. Yes, *eighty percent!* It's interesting to look at a few examples:

Aircraft	ROC	ROC S/E	% Loss
Beech B76 Duchess	1,248	235	81%
Beech B58 Baron	1,750	394	77%
Cessna 310	1,495	327	78%
Cessna 414	1,520	290	81%
Piper Seneca III	1,400	240	83%
Piper Navajo	1,670	325	81%
Average	**1,514**	**302**	**80%**

With an engine failure we lose 80% of rate of climb, therefore we are left with 20% or ⅕ of normal climb performance. So from 1,000 fpm rate of climb we are immediately reduced to 200 fpm and this is under *ideal* conditions. An older aircraft, heavily laden on a hot day out of Denver, may have a climb rate less than zero.

The decision is also one of steepness (gradient) as well as time (rate). We are used to being conscious of obstacles after takeoff and the use of maximum angle of climb V_X in these instances. We have been warned about the reduced margin of control above the stall and our vulnerability to gusts and downdrafts. Also at this lower speed, reaction time to lower the nose and maintain a safe glidespeed is critical. In a twin, we would only use the speed for maximum angle of climb if there was truly an obstacle in the after-takeoff climb area and we had no other choice.

However, certification requirements are predicated on the aircraft being able to achieve a certain *gradient* after takeoff, i.e. maximum angle of climb not maximum rate to clear terrain.

Effect of Wind on Climb Gradient

For safe terrain clearance VFR and IFR, the authority has chosen flightpaths which guarantee clearance for aircraft with 3% and 4% climb gradients respectively, all engines operating and for the single engine case, a gradient of 1% is required to be demonstrated at an altitude of 5,000 ft. All to do with *angle* of climb.

Further, we know that wind affects climb gradient or angle of climb. Climbing into wind gives a steeper path and better gradient. Conversely, turning downwind reduces the gradient. If we are considering a typical twin with a single engine best angle of climb airspeed, (V_{XSE}) of 70 kt and a rate of climb of 100 fpm, then a not uncommon 25 kt wind changes the gradient to 2% upwind and 1.1% downwind.

What does this mean to us? It means that the after-takeoff track is a crucial element in planning for an engine failure after takeoff (after we have the aircraft completely under control). It may be better to climb ahead to pattern altitude rather than turn downwind at the normal altitude—especially since turning also degrades climb performance—both angle and rate.

If we took off with a 20 kt crosswind from the left, then it is worth considering a very gentle turn to the left while climbing to take advantage of the increased gradient and airspeed. But think about this: we are flying below V_{IMD}, maximizing excess thrust, and we are not far above V_S. We are also close to V_{MC}. This is a danger *(high risk)* zone. All it needs is a gust of wind or a downdraft.

We can also use wind to our advantage in another way. By climbing into wind we can maintain the higher speed of V_{YSE}, realize a higher rate of climb and degree of controllability and still maintain an angle of climb equivalent to the no-wind gradient at V_{XSE}.

Wind has many faces when we are considering our actions—it can be very useful or very damaging depending on whether we are wise enough to take advantage of it. It can be friend or foe.

Conclusions

Performance Limitations Versus Handling Difficulties

Remember, V_{MC} and V_2 do not take into account any effect on performance i.e. whether the aircraft can maintain altitude, climb or turn. In any circumstances, control of the aircraft must be the first priority. However, after regaining control, we must consider the performance consequences. Thus the sequence of pilot actions in theory is simple:

- Establish control and carry out the immediate actions.
- Accelerate towards the recommended speed for the flight condition and the direction for best terrain clearance.
- Clean up the aircraft as you do so.
- When safely under control and clear of the ground tell someone—*Mayday* (but do not use the hand-held mike).
- Look after the good engine (*nurse it*).

These actions will be significantly improved in accuracy and response if rehearsed and self briefed before each takeoff. How do you convince someone to take that little extra time and trouble?

With an engine failure in a light twin we are going *nowhere*—unless the aircraft has been loaded to take this into account. Sounds serious—and it is. But we *could* load the aircraft like the *heavies* so that we have *acceptable* performance on one engine.

We can read back from the single engine climb performance graphs and load the aircraft to ensure at least a 2 or 3% climb gradient in the event of engine failure—even when the temperatures reaches 40°. Provided we are not trying to carry the maximum payload or to carry a full load and full fuel for a long sector, and if we are sufficiently current to quickly and correctly cope with the engine failure, we can build some performance margin. Ask your instructor about this option for your particular aircraft.

If you are prepared to stop for fuel en route or limit the payload, then you can always ensure *some* climb performance. And that is the way to operate. It can be a severe limitation in summer and there may be occasions where you will decide to take a calculated risk. As long as you are aware that in this case, an engine failure on takeoff is the same as a single—you have no option but to maintain directional control and use the engines to reach a suitable landing area. You can neither climb nor accelerate. You *must* land ahead.

Summary

There really are only two practicable options for control in the event of engine failure;
- the *wings-level* method which has advantages clear of the ground; and
- the *angle of bank* method which gives the maximum performance under the circumstances.

Performance is marginal in a light twin. It is vital to correctly identify the failed engine and feather the propeller. *Airspeed* is everything.

Chapter 5

Abnormal Operations

The Pilot's Operating Handbook for your aircraft will have the authoritative actions in the event of all abnormal and emergency operations. The following is a general introduction to the considerations and factors which should be taken into account.

Engine Start

Fire

Fire is the most serious event in an aircraft as there is little time to act. If there are positive indications or if you can see flames at all, get out as fast as you can and if you have a choice, exit via the door opposite to the burning engine (some twins have only one door but in this case, there should be an emergency exit via the pilot's side window).

If there are no flames but smoke or fumes from the intake or exhaust, it is worth briefly trying to suck the potential fire into the engine (which is designed for such high temperatures). Continue cranking the engine with the switches on, the throttle wide open and the mixture ICO. The engine will probably start with much billowing of blue smoke from the exhaust. When it starts, close the throttle and set the mixture to full rich. In this instance, the engine was probably hot and over-primed.

Hot Start

A hot start (as distinct from fire on start) is when you have just shut down on a very hot day and you need to re-start the engine soon after. The engine temperatures will actually have increased after shut down as a result of the residual heat in the engine compartments and the lack of cooling airflow from the propeller. The danger is over fuelling and fuel vaporization.

Your aircraft's flight manual should have hot start procedures but if not, first try starting without priming. If that is not immediately successful, try a normal start. Again if not successful try a start with no further priming but with the throttle fully open. Be ready to move the mixture to rich and the throttle to idle as soon as the engine starts.

Cold Start

Starting a cold engine is easier than a hot one—as there is little likelihood of over-priming. Rather there is a chance that you will not have provided enough fuel to balance the dense air and there is no chance of the engine starting under these circumstances. Try one normal start with the maximum recommended prime and if not successful, re-prime and try again. Under these circumstances, you can expect lots of blue smoke from the exhaust when the engine fires. On a very cold day use external power if you can. If not, start the first engine and run for five minutes or so with the alternator charging before trying to start the second engine.

Propeller Unfeather

If the engine had been shut down and feathered on the previous flight then you could encounter the situation of having to start with a feathered propeller. Check that the aircraft is serviceable? (The no-feather stop may not have operated on shut down.) Start normally but if the propeller doesn't move to a fine pitch position shortly after it starts rotating, then discontinue the start immediately.

Taxiing

Brake Failure

The circumstances of the failure will determine your actions, but do not continue to taxi. If you feel the loss of pressure in the pedal or that the brake is ineffective, close both throttles, both mixtures to ICO and try the parking brake if it is a separate system. If you are heading for a collision consider applying firm braking on the remaining wheel and using differential power to avoid collision.

Steering Failure

In the event of a failure of the nosewheel steering it is possible to steer by use of brakes and differential thrust. However, avoid confined spaces and do not taxi in close proximity to other aircraft, vehicles or buildings. It is preferable to simply taxi clear of the runways and taxiways and shut down.

Takeoff

Door Unlatch

Some aircraft are prone to the door becoming unlatched during the takeoff roll, if it hasn't been securely locked and checked prior to rolling. It is not a serious problem as long as you don't let it distract you from controlling the aircraft. If you haven't reached V_R, abort the takeoff, leave the runway, lock the door, repeat the pre-takeoff vital actions and start again.

If you have left the ground, ignore the door and fly the aircraft safely clear of the ground using normal checks and procedures. Don't try to reopen and close the door. Complete a normal pattern and land. If you have a passenger on that side of the aircraft, assure them that the door won't open and they won't be sucked out.

Aborted Takeoff

Discontinuing a takeoff is easy and safe—*if* the decision is made early. Close both throttles fully and apply the brakes firmly at first until you feel them biting and then reduce the pressure to allow them to cool as you slow down. Reapply the brakes as necessary.

Hold the control column back as it will reduce the load on the nosewheel and consequently help reduce the stress and maintain propeller clearance. Call *aborting* and try to stop on the runway. (If you are not using a headset, now is *not* the time to fumble for a microphone). If the runway length is marginal don't panic about stopping. The overruns are clear and it is preferable to leave the runway at slow speed under control rather than blow the tires or have smoking brakes and block the runway. If you need to shut down on the runway advise the tower.

Try to exit to one side and taxi slowly. If you stop and shut down and especially if you apply the parking brake, the residual heat can cause a fire or cause permanent damage to the brakes.

Continuing to taxi with minimum use of the brakes allows the air to cool them. Don't taxi close to other aircraft until you are sure that the brakes have cooled. There will be a noticeable smell from the overheated brakes and tires. If you think you have a brake fire, then shut down and leave the aircraft—after evacuating your passengers. Call the tower for assistance. Your cockpit fire extinguisher is not appropriate for the brake fire.

If you have to takeoff subsequent to an aborted takeoff (perhaps the unlatched door situation), then allow time for the brakes to cool before the second attempt. They need a good five minutes of taxiing or ten minutes stationary to cool. A second abort with hot brakes would place a major demand on them and there is a risk of the tire deflating.

Wet Runway—Hydroplaning

Low pressure tires can lose their grip of the runway at relatively low speeds. What happens is the water forms a layer of high pressure between the tire and the runway and if too much braking is applied, the aircraft starts to water-ski! The speed at which this happens is directly related to tire pressure by the formula, nine times the square root of the tire pressure in pounds per square inch (psi) so a big jet has an hydroplaning speed (the speed above which it will hydroplane if the wheels lock) of 90 kt or more (100 psi tire pressure) and a light twin, a speed of about 54 kt (36 psi or so).

The larger aircraft has anti-skid brakes which release the brake pressure if the wheel slows down or stops. Small twins have no such system and it is up to the pilot to sense when the wheels are skidding and to momentarily release the brake application. Also when landing on a wet runway, braking should be delayed until the aircraft is below hydroplaning speed.

Wheelbarrowing

There is a tendency for all aircraft to *wheelbarrow*. This is a condition where the aircraft has reached flying speed and too much forward pressure is being applied deliberately or inadvertently, to the control column and this is preventing the aircraft from becoming airborne. This upload on the horizontal stabilizer and the lift generated by the wings, reduces the weight on the main wheels and increases the weight on the nosewheel.

The reason a pilot may deliberately hold the aircraft down is to reach V_{MC} before becoming airborne and so create a margin of safety. Unfortunately, the nosewheel is not designed for such loads and the geometry of the landing gear is such that directional control can be lost and the nosewheel could collapse sideways.

It is safer to fly the aircraft into the air and allow it to accelerate in ground effect with the landing gear down until the decision point or decision speed is reached.

Wheelbarrowing can also occur on landing if the aircraft is put onto the ground before it has assumed a tail down attitude—i.e. at too high a speed.

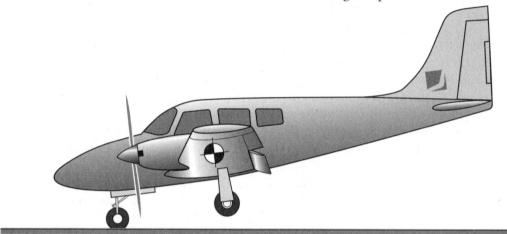

■ **Wheelbarrowing**

Engine Failure/Loss of Thrust on Takeoff

Choosing the Decision Point or Speed

Speeds for our Bushcraft are as follows:

V_{MC}	65 KIAS
V_{S1}	70 KIAS
V_R	71 KIAS
V_{YSE}	85 KIAS

Stall speed V_{S1} is with power off but in the event of engine failure, that is exactly the state of that wing. We need to choose a liftoff speed to give ourselves a margin of safety over both V_{MC} and V_S.

$1.1 \times V_{MC}$	= 72 KIAS	$1.1 \times V_{S1}$	= 77 KIAS
$1.15 \times V_{MC}$	= 75 KIAS	$1.15 \times V_{S1}$	= 81 KIAS
$1.2 \times V_{MC}$	= 78 KIAS	$1.2 \times V_{S1}$	= 84 KIAS

We now have to consider wheelbarrowing and other problems associated with keeping the aircraft on the ground above the speed at which it wants to fly. Leaving the flaps up for takeoff will certainly help. Unless field length is critical it would be reasonable to begin rotation at 75 KIAS to achieve lift off at 80 KIAS. If there is further runway available we could accept a later point beyond which we are committed to go. It could be a physical feature on the runway.

Maintain a shallow climb until through 85 KIAS and if there is no excess runway remaining in front, select gear up—and like Jodie Foster, you are *"GO."* You will hear reference to V_1 as decision speed. This decision speed is the last speed at which you can still safely abort the takeoff within the remaining length of the runway. It is relevant to large aircraft because a *Jumbo* running off the end of the runway with smoking brakes is a serious matter.

Conversely, a Jumbo continuing a takeoff after engine failure at V_1 is not a problem. It is easy to control and has guaranteed climb performance. Airline crews practice V_1 cuts regularly (in the full flight simulator).

Do you see the different emphasis between the Jumbo and our twin?

Pre-Decision Point or Speed

We have discussed the concepts of decision point and decision speed. In either case, an engine failure before reaching this point or speed is a *no questions asked,* aborted takeoff. Immediately close both throttles and proceed for the aborted takeoff. There will be no problems with directional control as long as both throttles are closed. Don't try to diagnose the problem or which engine has failed, simply keep straight, close the throttles and start braking.

Pre-Decision Point and Airborne

There can be a situation where the aircraft is airborne, accelerating in ground effect, the landing gear is down and the engine fails. Again a relatively simple matter of keeping straight, closing both throttles, allowing the nose to drop to maintain airspeed and to descend to the runway. There may be time to select full flap but do not be concerned. Concentrate on a normal landing and don't force the aircraft onto the ground. If you run off the end of the runway, so be it.

The awkward situation arises if you have selected the landing gear up before this point. If so, you can close the throttles and select the gear down in the hope it will extend before touch down or leave it up and land wheels-up. Hence the importance of being disciplined to delay landing gear retraction until committed to go. There can be a ludicrous situation on a 10,000 ft runway where it is silly to leave the landing gear retraction until near the end and to delay any potential climb and acceleration for this time. Retract the gear no later than V_{YSE} and regard the selection as a *go* commitment.

Post-Decision Point/Post Landing Gear Up Selection

This is the critical one. Engine failure at this stage must be handled quickly and correctly. The decision has already been made to go—no questions asked any more. You have selected gear up. The propeller mechanism includes a stop pin that prevents feathering below a certain RPM, typically about 900 RPM. This was discussed in the description of the system in Chapter One.

A typical light twin at V_{YSE} has a propeller windmilling RPM of about 1,500 so its not a problem. But below this speed, the consequence of a failure is that the pilot must identify and confirm that it is a total failure, confirm the failed engine and select feather before the speed further reduces—a big ask. (Yet another reason to delay the go/no go decision until landing gear selection at V_{YSE} and not before.)

The safest action on detecting significant yaw and loss of thrust, is to assume engine failure and carry out the full procedure immediately.

Let's go through it.

- Keep looking ahead.
- Stop the yaw.
- Stop the roll and then bank slightly towards the live engine.
- Hold a level attitude (level flight attitude, that is—about 7° nose-up, but use a visual reference).
- Now that you are in control, carry out the immediate actions.

Pitch up, mixtures up, power up, gear up, flap up is a commonly taught litany. The reference is to propeller pitch being selected to full fine—not to be confused with the term *pitch* as in pitch attitude. It may seem that the full procedure is a little meaningless as you have just taken off on full power (full throttle, propellers fully fine and mixtures rich). Now you know why the hand is held across the levers—you know you have full power, you know you have selected gear up and you are committed to go. The gear was selected up at the decision point, so really, all that's left is the flaps. Most light twins don't use flaps for a normal takeoff and we have discussed the advantage of not using flaps for a normal takeoff anyway. If you do, selecting it up when the aircraft is just out of ground effect and before reaching climb speed, leaves a risk of settling. You don't want to have to increase the angle of attack to compensate while you are trying to accelerate to V_{YSE}. So leave the flaps alone.

The reason that many instructors teach the full procedure described above is because it covers all situations and they are trying to establish a conditioned response. However, it is also not entirely appropriate in the cruise or the descent. In fact, it is only totally applicable in the climb. In the takeoff situation, forget about all of the other *levers and pulleys*. Get the aircraft under control, identify the failed engine (dead leg, left leg, left engine identified—move the throttle and check no noise variation and no yaw, left engine confirmed, left engine feather.)

The response to engine failure on takeoff has to be quick, consistent and correct. It is vital that you discuss this aspect thoroughly with your instructor and then practice the procedure for your aircraft.

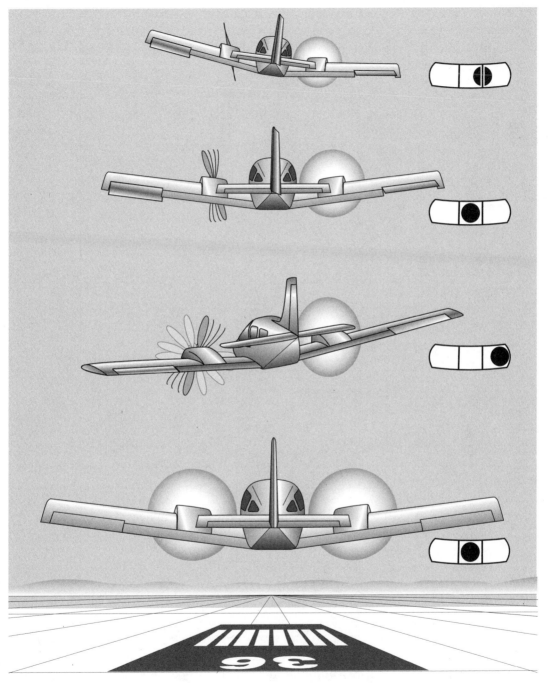

■ **Engine failure after takeoff (EFATO)**

Don't be rushed. It takes 20–30 seconds for the aircraft to slow from 100 kt to 85 kt, so there is adequate time to carry out the actions. Rehearse the procedure so that you can do the actions at the same speed as you would say them, at a normal conversational speed.

■ **Engine failure—go**

The rhythm or cadence is important. Once again, say aloud:
- *engine failure* (stop the yaw);
- *dead leg* (the dead leg is the relaxed, soft or non-pushing leg but in the circumstances you may be tense as a result of the emergency);
- *left leg* (wiggle it, even move it off the rudder pedal and watch that the heading doesn't change);
- *left engine* (left throttle—move it forward and back—no response—no yaw, look outside);

- *left engine confirmed* (hand on left propeller lever);
- *left engine-feather;*
- *performance* (accelerating to Blue Line, if not, then the pitch attitude has to be lowered until it does accelerate);
- *decision* (Can the aircraft climb away from here? Is the aircraft accelerating? Is the aircraft climbing? If no, to both, then look for somewhere *in the forward field of view*, to land. If the failed propeller is feathered and the aircraft is loaded correctly, it should climb under any circumstances. If you don't fly regularly, then this is the procedure to practice aloud in your lounge room and in the cockpit before engine start.)

Remember that it can take as much as 150 lb foot force to stop the yaw at V_{MC}. So we could have close to this force at V_{TOSS}. You will have considerable reaction against the back of your seat as you push hard on the rudder pedal. It is a crucial pre-takeoff vital action to include seat position for full rudder deflection and that the seat is positively locked. It can be included under the caption "Hatches and Harnesses—Secure."

Engine Failure in the Climb

Once the aircraft is established in the climb at V_Y, engine failure is not such a serious concern. It's a matter of maintaining control and then maintaining V_{YSE}.

Depending on altitude, the checks can be done without too much haste. The aircraft is in a climb configuration with gear and flaps up but with climb power set. So, once control is established and the nose is lowered to maintain V_{YSE}, go through the complete sequence of immediate actions. Allow the aircraft to accelerate. V_Y and V_{YSE} are usually very close to the same speed so lowering the pitch attitude to level will be sufficient. Then declare an emergency and secure the failed engine.

Engine Failure in the Cruise

Unlike engine failure on takeoff or during the initial climb when the failure is likely to be sudden and irretrievable, total or partial engine failure in the cruise is more likely as a result of fuel starvation, carburetor icing or low oil pressure. There is some time for fault diagnosis and once control is established, you should carry out the recommended actions to turn the boost pump on, change fuel selection, mixture rich and select carb heat on before feathering the propeller. Windmilling RPM should stay above 1,500 so there is no urgency to feather, but check the figure for your aircraft.

Actions
Engine Indications
Engine failure in the cruise is not violent. At higher levels the MP will remain around the cruise setting (approx. 20 inches) and RPM will decay slowly. While there is oil pressure, the CSU will sense the decaying RPM and will move the blades to fine pitch. If oil pressure is lost, the blades go to full coarse. At lower altitudes the MP may increase

to about 25 inches. EGT will drop quickly with engine failure whereas CHT and oil temperature will fall slowly.

What power to set on the live engine? Obviously, if you have 23 inches and 2,300 RPM when an engine fails, then going suddenly to full power on the live engine can cause more problems than it solves. You only need enough to maintain speed and altitude. As a guide, go to the next one up, i.e. if climbing—set full power, if cruising—set climb power, if descending—set cruise power. This will give sufficient without being too much. Close the cowl flap of the failed engine to reduce drag. Now it becomes time to nurse the live engine. Reduce the power when you can and ensure the cowl flap is open. Head for home. Monitor CHT and oil temperature. Use the rudder trim to reduce your foot loads—again always look outside to maintain direction as you do it. *Live leg, live engine, live trim,* i.e. if the left leg is pushing, move the rudder trim to the left.

Assuming an engine failure (or loss of oil pressure—in which case, you have to shut it down anyway), decide on your destination and tell someone. Once established en route, fuel management becomes a consideration, especially if you are still some distance from your destination or departure airfield. Now is the time to be familiar (not to *become* familiar) with your aircraft's fuel system. Don't do anything that may interrupt fuel to the live engine! Crossfeed to retrieve fuel from the dead tank but be cautious in your selection. Turn on the boost pump as recommended.

As you may have some distance to go before landing, you will need to nurse the live engine. Monitor the temperatures and use minimum power to reach your destination. Reduce the electrical load to essential items. Open the cowl flap and enrich the mixture before reducing airspeed or descending—if that is recommended by the Pilot's Operating Handbook. If conditions warrant it, select carburetor heat to hot. If the engine is turbocharged make a minimal power adjustment for descent. Plan a normal, cruise descent at normal cruise speed—if you know that the weather on arrival will be OK.

Plan to arrive over the destination airfield with altitude to spare, say 2,000 ft and then the rejoin will be relaxed as far as the power required is concerned. If the destination is likely to be IMC then stay above the lowest safe altitude and ask for radar guidance.

Use of Trim

Once the aircraft is under control and the performance is adequate then you can relieve the personal tension by trimming out the asymmetric forces. There is no problem with this as long as you remember to keep the aircraft straight during the landing flare as the rudder trim will be working against you. Alternatively, center the rudder trim on final when you make the commitment to land.

Use of Autopilot

If the failure occurred when the aircraft was on autopilot, it should have automatically disconnected. If not, be careful when you do—as it could be holding significant out-of-trim forces. Once the asymmetric condition is controlled, then there is no reason not to use the autopilot to help you fly home. Depending on the autopilot authority, it may not be able to be engaged until all the out-of-trim forces are manually removed. Be careful of the altitude hold mode. If the engine fails, the autopilot will struggle to maintain altitude and airspeed will be compromised. Be careful if you had altitude hold before the engine failure. The autopilot will accept an airspeed decay to maintain altitude.

Effect of Engine Failure on Other Systems

Fuel. Can you access all of the remaining fuel? Can you balance the aircraft laterally or will there be a significant fuel imbalance for landing. It may be appropriate to carefully carry out a low speed handling check to ensure that there is sufficient aileron power at approach speed before you descend from a safe altitude.

Oil. As well as the need to monitor temperature and pressure, check that under these circumstances, the endurance is not limited by oil consumption.

Electrical. Reduce the load but also check if your aircraft has specific limits when one alternator is operating. There may be a maximum electrical load.

Vacuum. Vacuum pressure should be maintained on one engine but keep an eye on it. The primary instruments and autopilot need it.

Loss of Oil Pressure. A loss of oil pressure suggests a precautionary shut down and feather before the centrifugal latch prevents feathering.

Pressurization. Cabin pressure should be maintained by one engine.

Engine Failure in the Descent

Engine failure during a cruise descent is not a serious issue and it may even go unnoticed until it comes time to level off when power is re-introduced. Simply keep straight and increase power on the live engine to maintain your profile.

Engine Failure During the Approach

The second worst time to have an engine failure is when you are on final in the landing configuration with full flap and you are below glidepath and, heaven forbid, slow.

Increase to climb power (pitch levers and mixtures should already be full forward) while watching for any yaw that can't be contained with full rudder and while maintaining a downward flightpath. Select flap to takeoff. Do not try to go round from here but accept a touchdown short of the threshold. Once the airspeed is increasing, the power can be further increased. Again watch for any yaw that you can't contain.

As soon as you feel that you have reached the limit of rudder power, leave the throttles and accept the flightpath. The likelihood is that once you are in ground effect, you will reach the runway anyway. If the undershoot area is obstructed, select gear up and try to reach the threshold for a wheels-up landing. Don't bother with the identify, confirm, feather process. There are more important things to be done.

Engine Failure During Normal Go-around

Engine failure during go-around is as bad or worse than engine failure on takeoff. When you have set full power on both engines to go-around, the gear and flaps are still down and one engine suddenly and completely fails it's a difficult situation. It's a hard one to call because it depends if the runway is still available and what altitude you have. As a general rule, treat it like a takeoff, so if the gear is down land ahead. If the gear is selected up, lower the nose to maintain speed and clean up.

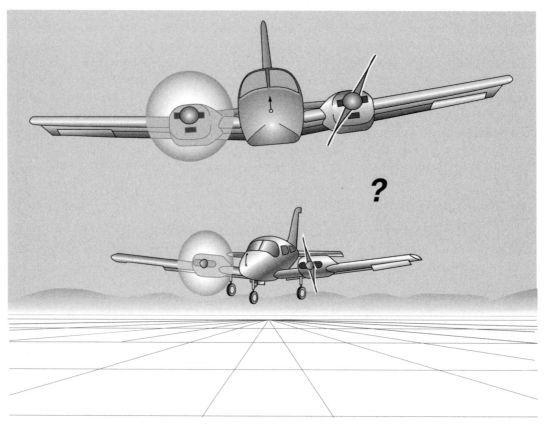

■ **Engine failure during normal go-around**

Asymmetric Pattern

If you have had an engine failure and secured the engine, you will join the pattern for a landing with one engine inoperative. The main criterion is not to let yourself get into a position of being committed to land until you are certain of reaching the threshold.

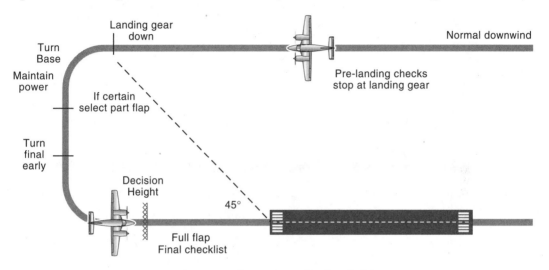

■ Asymmetric pattern—Bushcraft 71

Let's consider the rejoin and arrival. Join the pattern for a normal spacing and carry out the pre-landing checks except leave the landing gear up. Turn base in the normal position and select landing gear down at this point.

Leave the flaps up. Aim to intercept the normal glidepath and if anything, err on the high side. Don't become low and don't allow speed to come below V_{YSE} or V_{MC} + 10 kt until the final commitment to land.

On final and before 300 ft AGL (preferably earlier), decide whether to continue or not. Once this commitment is made then do not attempt to go-around. So, leave the selection of full flaps until this point or leave them at the lesser setting. Below 300 ft, you are *committed* to a landing.

Asymmetric Go-around

If you are not continuing—and it would have to be a bl★★★y good reason—select full power and maintain the approach attitude while watching for any yaw that can't be controlled.

When you reach full power or full rudder (whichever occurs first), select gear up and as the airspeed increases, increase to full power. At V_{YSE} transition to a single-engine climb occurs. Climb straight ahead to normal pattern altitude. Don't turn early and don't turn downwind—choose a turn direction into wind if possible.

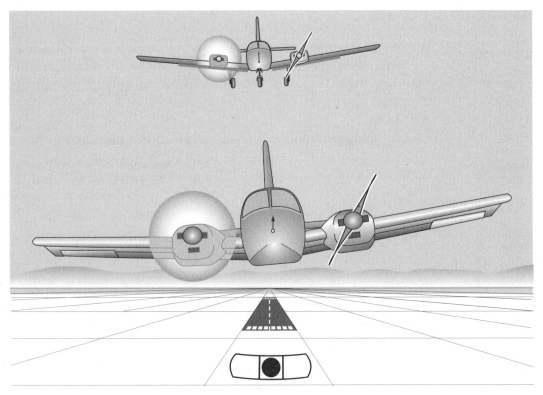

■ **Going around—decide before full flap extension**

Asymmetric Landing

Assuming you arrive at your decision height of 300 ft and it looks good, then continue. Select full flap (or leave it set where it is), complete the final (PUF) check and say to yourself, *"I am now committed to land"*—and that means *committed*. You *do not* go-around. If the runway is obstructed, land on the parallel taxiway or on the grass next to the runway. If you decide to commit to a landing before 300 ft and lower the flap, then that becomes your committal point. Reduce now to normal approach speed and center the rudder trim for landing. Fly a normal approach profile at normal speeds. Don't add a few knots for the kids. Be careful of crosswind. Use the crab technique. The controls are crossed enough as it is. A wing down side slipping approach may compound the problem. Keep the ball centered—use rudder with power changes.

In the flare, you will need to concentrate on keeping straight as you reduce power to idle. Also you may have forgotten to center the rudder trim. Thus in the flare, as you reduce the live engine to idle, the rudder trim will be too powerful and you will need to override it with rudder. Treat it like a crosswind landing. Look well ahead and keep straight until touchdown.

Fire In Flight

The most serious and most urgent emergency that you can have is a fire in flight. If there is a fire warning light with no other symptoms, then initially take no action but monitor everything very closely and look for the slightest confirmation of a fire. Turn towards the nearest airfield though. If there is a fire, there are likely to be other engine indications (but not necessarily, e.g. if an exhaust manifold has come adrift) such as rough running or RPM fluctuations, unusual electrical system indications, circuit breakers popping etc. Finally there may be a visible indication such a smoke or fumes.

If there is any symptom that is unusual, shut down the engine, cut off the fuel to that engine and turn off that alternator. Again look for signs of fire. If there are visible signs then you must act very quickly. Establish an emergency descent and land in *any* suitable area—and do it quickly. A fire in the engine compartment can burn through the magnesium alloy wing structure in a matter of a few minutes.

Propeller No Unfeather

Some small twins don't have an unfeathering accumulator. In this case, if a practice feathering has been carried out an airstart may be necessary. Also it is possible that even with an accumulator, the prop will not come out of the feather position. The worst situation that you will have will be a pre-planned and controlled, single-engine approach and landing.

Engine Restart in Flight

If the engine has stopped due to a known cause such as fuel exhaustion of one tank (which of course should never happen) there will be a simple restart procedure. Allow several minutes at low power for the temperatures to rise before demanding high power settings. This is equally important for practice shut downs.

Taxiing on One Engine

Avoid taxiing on one engine except to clear the runway.

Propeller Runaway

A propeller over-speed where the RPM governor lets go is very rare. A situation that is more likely, is a temporary overspeed if the power is increased too rapidly or the engine is restarted in flight with the throttle wide open. What to do? Simply retard the throttle to idle and the propeller lever to mid-way. If this doesn't reduce the RPM, shut down the engine and feather the propeller. Declare an emergency.

Stall/Spin

If the aircraft departs from controlled flight for any reason, *stop the yaw* and if you reach full rudder, reduce the power—even if you are heading for the ground. Centralize the control column (remove any back pressure and the wing will be unstalled). If the aircraft auto rotates, close both throttles apply full opposite rudder and move the control column forward. Hold until the spin stops.

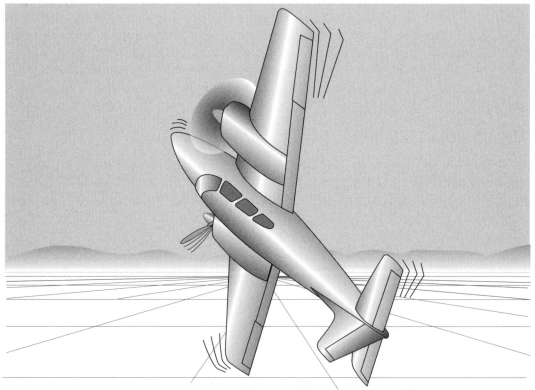

■ **Stall from asymmetric flight**

If you stall from an asymmetric condition, close both throttles and lower the nose immediately as you stop the yaw. Retract the landing gear and flap.

Bird Strike

The main decision with regard to a bird strike is to assess whether it has or will, come through the windscreen or the engine/propeller, or impact the flight controls—and what will be the consequences. Avoid going under the bird since there is more likelihood of a strike as they tend to dive for the ground when they see or hear you. Try to go over him, her or them. If it is heading for your eyes, raise the nose and if necessary, yaw the aircraft slightly to avoid a direct impact on the windscreen.

Don't do any air show maneuvers or violent turns. Simply raise the nose and sideslip a little. If you have high power set and can temporarily do without it, then retard the throttles before the impact.

After any strike, watch out for erroneous airspeed readings in case the pitot head has been damaged. Always set attitude and power that you know. Watch out for asymmetric flap. If you suspect airframe damage reduce to V_{YSE} at a safe altitude and check the aircraft's behavior. Use this as your minimum approach speed.

Takeoff Roll. A strike during the takeoff roll is an immediate abort. No questions asked.

After Takeoff. Takeoff is the critical time—and the very situation where you can't afford to try and pass under the birds. Maintain the attitude and power and pass through. Keep climbing and watch for signs of damage. If there is any engine/propeller vibration gradually reduce the throttles individually to climb power and be ready for any signs of the vibration worsening. If it does, there is no choice but to continue the power reduction on that engine and if the vibration becomes severe, immediately retard the throttle to idle and feather the engine.

Climb. Bird impact in the climb if well clear of the ground is best treated by lowering the nose and a consequent reduction in power. Then decide on the seriousness of the situation. Watch for engine indications if there was a chance that it went down the intake or through the propeller.

Cruise. If there is a strike in the cruise slow down and return to land. Keep speeds below V_A and power at or below cruise settings. (Yes, birds fly at high altitudes.)

Approach. On final, you have nowhere to go as far as bird strike avoidance is concerned. You can't afford to maneuver violently at low speed, low power and low altitude. Continue the approach, take the hits and reach the runway.

Fuel System

Probably the most common cause of major accidents in twins is not mechanical failure of an engine but incorrect management of fuel and the serious consequences (including engine failure on one or both sides) that result from such mismanagement. A wise old pilot gave two pieces of advice to an aspiring multi-engine pilot. They were:

• Practice engine failure drills until they become second nature.
• Learn the fuel system so that you always know what you have remaining, in which tanks, and how to get every gallon of fuel for either engine, as you need it.

Electrical System

An electrical failure as a consequence of an engine or alternator failure is not too serious but you may have to turn off non-essential services. A total electrical failure is unlikely but can happen. With both alternators out, you can expect manual landing gear extension, no landing gear downlights, a flapless approach and a no landing-light, no radio landing. Conserve battery power. Assume that no one will see or hear you and make allowances. Double check that the runway is clear before landing.

Landing Gear

Manual extension of the landing gear depends on whether the gear actuation is totally by electric motor or by an electrically driven hydraulic pump. The former may require you to crank the gear down by 50–60 rotations of a handle which could be on the floor in the rear. In the case of the hydraulic system, you can simply unlock the gear and allow it to drop to the down position. Check your aircraft's system because an engine failure may deplete the electrical supply and it may take some time to crank the gear down when you need it. You may need to allow a few minutes to get the gear down. Not easy when you are in IMC.

Wheels Up Landing (All or Some)

Carry out a normal approach but allow for less drag. As you start to flare retard the throttles, select propellers to feather, mixtures to ICO and hold off normally. Allow the aircraft to settle until prop contact. Try to keep straight and to keep the nose up.

Depressurization/Emergency Descent

Your aircraft will have specific actions in the event of depressurization but in essence, return to altitudes below 10,000 ft, as soon as is safely practicable. Secure your quick-donning oxygen mask and check the oxygen flow, before you do anything else. Then head downhill. Then look after your passengers.

Be careful about how you handle an emergency descent. Entry needs to be quick but not violent. The rate of descent will necessarily be high but the airspeed must be closely observed. If possible, stay below V_A if there is any turbulence. Lower the landing gear if needed to control speed. Lower the nose, propellers to fine pitch, throttles to idle. During the descent watch out for reduced visibility due to condensation in hot, humid conditions.

Icing

As soon as ice starts to build (probably wing leading edges) ask for a change of cruising level (up or down), clear of cloud and terrain. If not available ask for a diversion from cloud and high terrain. Turn the pitot and carburetor heat on. Monitor engine parameters. Allow the ice to form a hard crust before operating the boots. Actuate the windscreen demist well before descent point.

Flight in Turbulence

If there is any turbulence, the maximum speed is V_A. Below this speed, there is a protection against structural failure. Any vertical gusts or sudden control deflections will cause a stall before reaching the structural load limit. The most vulnerable time is descending at V_{NO} and approaching uneven terrain, or approaching lower altitudes when the surface wind is high or where thermal activity may be pronounced. Anticipate the effect and at least reduce the airspeed from V_{NO} before the turbulence.

Your passengers will be very concerned about turbulence and will feel it more strongly in the cabin—especially if they are not expecting it. There will be a more pronounced yawing and rolling motion associated with turbulence as seen from the rear of the aircraft. You won't feel it as badly as your pax. Assure them that all is under control.

Wake Turbulence

Wake turbulence from a large aircraft or helicopter, can take you beyond the limits of control of your twin. Treat a large aircraft like a large bird and don't fly below its flightpath. The minimum time delay for dissipation of the vortices is recommended as 3 minutes.

If you have to takeoff behind a jet, liftoff early and climb before the jet's liftoff point and turn before you reach the jet's climb path (preferably towards the upwind side). On landing, land further into the field and don't forget that the jet will have used an aim point 1,000 ft in from the threshold. Stay above this approach path.

Windshear

Momentum is the problem. We were taught that the aircraft flies in a parcel of air and that it doesn't matter what that parcel is doing, our airspeed through it stays the same. This is true except when we move from one parcel to another. During the transition, the aircraft retains its momentum relative to the earth until the new aerodynamic forces come into play. With a small aircraft that happens fairly quickly as they have little momentum. However, it can be embarrassing near the ground.

In the case of a large aircraft, the transition takes a finite and serious period of time. Let's consider a few scenarios.

You are taking off from a short strip with a strong, 20 kt crosswind. You adopt the short takeoff technique and plan to climb at V_X, which in this example is 68 kt. V_S is 62 kt, power off with takeoff flap. You liftoff as planned and establish an obstacle clearance climb. The wind is gusty and the airspeed is fluctuating plus and minus 5 kt. Your clearance of high ground is marginal and so you turn right, away from the terrain feature.

As you turn from runway heading you are changing from a situation where your airspeed is 68 kt and your groundspeed is 68 kt to a situation where your momentum (remember, momentum is mass times velocity where velocity is in space i.e. groundspeed) maintains the 68 kt energy level but momentarily, you have lost some of its 20 kt of airspeed! Although full power is set, the drag at this reduced airspeed is actually higher than it was at 68 kt and to accelerate quickly you may have to lower the nose. Hopefully you have enough altitude to do it. Watch out for the downdraft in the lee of the hill!

Another situation plagues the big jets. Let's say the jet is established on final at 3,000 ft with ten miles to run to touchdown. There is a headwind at this altitude of 20 kt changing to a crosswind from the left at 1,500 ft and no wind at surface level.

Let's see what happens to the airspeed and the groundspeed. At 3,000 ft the pilot has established V_{REF} plus 10, say 150 kt. Groundspeed (momentum) is 130 kt. As it approaches 1,500 ft, the momentum of 130 kt is maintained. It takes a large force to quickly change the momentum of a Jumbo.

As the wind changes from a headwind to a crosswind it suddenly loses 20 kt of airspeed. The pilot increases thrust and monitors the rate of descent. As the aircraft accelerates back to V_{REF}, the windshear takes a change for the worse and momentarily there is a tailwind at 500 ft. Once again the airspeed falls and the aircraft is perilously close to the ground. Even with anticipation and increasing thrust it is awkward to be fighting these changes while trying to stabilize the approach to land. This could well end with an exceedingly heavy landing as the airspeed reduction may result in insufficient airspeed to arrest the rate of descent.

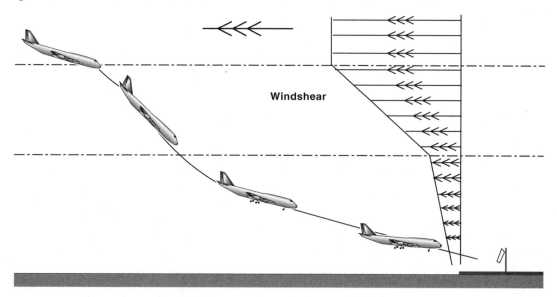

Windshear

■ The danger of a reducing headwind

Don't be caught short. If you have a situation developing like this, don't chase airspeed. Maintain attitude and increase if necessary to full power. If necessary, retract the landing gear and bring the flaps up in stages to takeoff and then up. Don't turn except to avoid high ground. Don't turn downwind. In the worst case, you will arrest the descent in ground effect.

Chapter 6

Performance and Flight Planning

Operating a twin-engine aircraft, places a greater onus on the pilot to pre-calculate the performance parameters before getting airborne. The successful and safe completion of a flight ultimately depends on these performance calculations.

In the single you may have adopted the habit of always filling the fuel tanks. Some pilots would say that it is good airmanship to always carry full fuel unless the payload doesn't allow it. In the twin you should *never* carry full fuel.

Always calculate the required flight fuel plus reserves and take no more. Any additional fuel is literally dead weight. Leave it behind.

When you plan your flight in a twin, there are many factors to be taken into account and unfortunately it is not just a matter of reading data from the charts in the Pilot's Operating Handbook.

You do have to go one step further as I will explain.

We will consider all of the factors in turn. Of course if you are flying a standard aircraft in your local training area from your known airfield in a standard configuration with a standard fuel load, then you do not have to recalculate every time (indeed it is useful to prepare your own summary of performance parameters for the standard configurations that you use).

But as soon as one of the variables changes, you would be wise to run through the full set of performance calculations.

The problem is further compounded by the various units of measurement used in the world of aviation. Be very careful about the units you are using.

Never write down a number without units alongside.

Once again we will refer to the Bushcraft 71. Its Pilot's Operating Handbook uses units of U.S. gallons (USG), pounds (lb), feet and inches (in.).

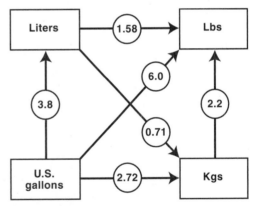

To convert:
- follow the arrow and multiply
- backtrack the arrow and divide

■ **Conversion table for AVGAS**

By way of illustrating the factors to be considered in planning a cross-country flight we will plan a theoretical flight from Canberra (Australia's capital) to Melbourne (capital of the southern state of Victoria). The route takes us over Australia's highest mountain range—the Snowy mountains.

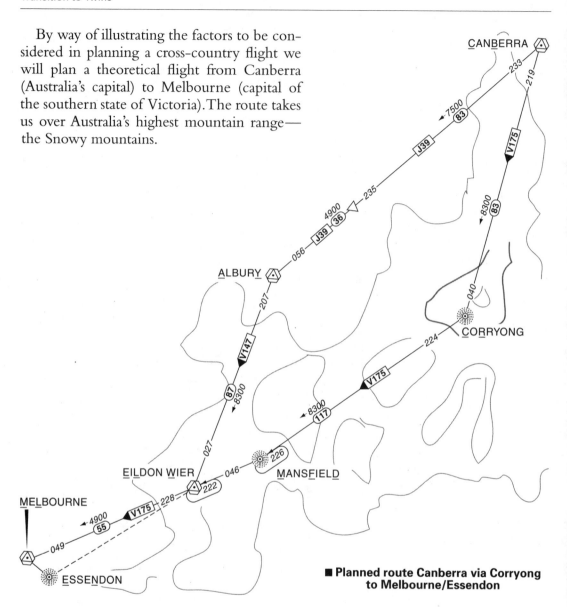

■ Planned route Canberra via Corryong to Melbourne/Essendon

Aircraft Type	Bushcraft BC 71
Pilot Weight	198 lb
Passenger—Front Seat	189 lb
Passengers—Rear seats two at	308 lb
Baggage—overnight bags	187 lb

For small aircraft always weigh or at least assess the weight of each of the passengers. Don't use a standard weight, it's not accurate enough for our critical performance margins.

Planned Flight

The route will be Canberra–Corryong–Mansfield–Eildon Weir–ML–Essendon, on ATS route V175.

Lowest Safe Altitude (LSALT)

Lowest safe altitude provides at least 1,000 ft clearance above the highest terrain or obstacle. The highest LSALT for this sector is 8,300 ft due to the Snowy Mountains. It is probably the most severe sector for light aircraft. In winter, there is a serious risk of carburetor and even airframe icing. Yet it is a much travelled route. You will note that there is another track via Albury with a lowest safe altitude of 7,500 ft. However, via Corryong is the shortest distance so let's consider going via CRG but keep in mind Albury as an option.

Canberra Details

ATIS CANBERRA
"Canberra Terminal Information Delta,
Runway 35,
Wind 320/ 15 KNOTS,
Altimeter 1023 Hpa (30.21 in.),
TEMPERATURE 36°C,
CAVOK"
(Runway length in metres.)

AREA and TERMINAL FORECASTS

AREA30 (Covering the whole flight)

AMENDED AREA FORECAST 062200 TO 071900 AREA 30

SUBDIVISION:
AREA A. NORTH OF a line between COOMA/ALBURY
AREA B. SOUTH OF a line between COOMA/ALBURY

WIND:	2000 ft	5000 ft	7000 ft	10000 ft	14000 ft
AREA A.	300/25	270/30	260/35	260/45 MS02	270/60 MS09
AREA B.	190/25	230/30	240/30	240/40 MS07	250/40 MS15

MELBOURNE FIR (YMMM)

SIGMET NIL

ALBURY (YMAY) (Aerodrome Forecast)

TAF YMAY 062200Z 2406 26010KT 9999 FEW045 (Patches of cloud 4500 ft) SCT100 (Scattered Cloud 1000 ft)

T (Temperatures °Celsius) 15 17 15 12 (= 60 64 60 54 °Fahrenheit)
Q (Altimeter) 1008 1007 1006 1006 (29.77 → 29.71 in.)

CANBERRA AIRPORT
(runway length in meters)

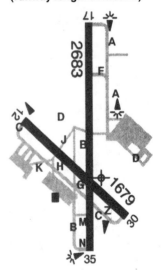

Cruising Levels

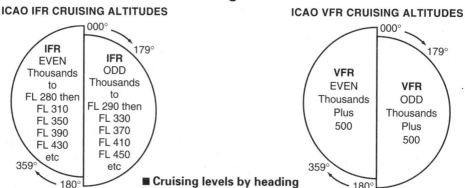

ICAO IFR CRUISING ALTITUDES

000°
IFR EVEN Thousands to FL 280 then FL 310 FL 350 FL 390 FL 430 etc
IFR ODD Thousands to FL 290 then FL 330 FL 370 FL 410 FL 450 etc
179°
359°
180°

■ **Cruising levels by heading**

ICAO VFR CRUISING ALTITUDES

000°
VFR EVEN Thousands Plus 500
VFR ODD Thousands Plus 500
179°
359°
180°

As shown, the lowest cruising level VFR above the lowest safe altitude is 8,500 ft.

Recommended Cruise

From the performance chart for the Bushcraft at the chosen cruising level we will use a recommended cruise power setting of 24 in. (or full throttle) 2,300 RPM.

MELBOURNE / Essendon

17
1585
1921
08
26
35

Melbourne/Essendon Details

ESSENDON (YMEN)

TAF

TAF YMEN 062300Z 2406 24020G30KT 8500 BKN015 (Broken cloud 1500 ft) OVC030 (Overcast 3000 ft)

INTER (30 minutes holding fuel required) 0911 4000 +SHRA SCT010 (showers)

T 17 18 19 18 Q 1004 1005 1006 1006

(Runway length in meters.)

Planned Cruise

Canberra–Corryong

83 NM   Tr 219 M   LSALT 8,300 ft

Corryong–Eildon Weir

117 NM   Tr 224 M   LSALT 8,300 ft

Eildon Weir–Melbourne/Essendon

55 NM   Tr 228 M   LSALT 4,900 ft

Full throttle at 8,500 ft is 21.5 in. at 2,300 RPM uses 8.65 gals/hr per engine (17.3 gal/hr total). This gives an indicated airspeed of 132 kt and a true airspeed of 155 kt, (132 KIAS, 155 KTAS).

Flight Planning Sequence

Let's start at the beginning. We wish to carry our passengers and baggage from Canberra to Melbourne. The first question we must answer is, *"can we carry them and sufficient fuel for the flight or will we have to stop on the way?"* The first step then is to calculate the required fuel for the flight with adequate reserves. From the area weather forecast, (FA), we can determine an average wind velocity (W/V) at 8,500 ft to be 250°/40 kt. The average temperature en route, at 10,000 ft is −5°C, which is equivalent to ISA for that level. Therefore at 8,500 ft, the temperature to use will be −2°C.

For the climb from Canberra, we can use the wind at 5,000 ft (⅔ height for the climb) in Subdivision A of Area 30, to establish the wind component to apply to the still air data. We'll use 270/30 kt. For the descent into Essendon we can interpolate in Subdivision B for 4,000 ft (the ½ way height), and use 220/30 kt. (Remember that these winds are expressed in °True.) The terminal forecast (TAF) for Essendon shows that during the period covering our expected arrival time (ETA), there is an operational requirement for 30 minutes holding (INTER).

Climb

For the climb the track is 219°M with a variation of 12°E. This gives a true track of 231° and a headwind component of 22 kt.

Press Alt	Time	Fuel	Dist
8,500	10.5	5.0	19.0
2,000	1.5	1.0	2.5
∴ climb to cruise level	9.0 min	4.0 USG	16.5 ANM
wind effect 22 kt HEAD			
for	9.0 min		−3.5
			13.0 GNM

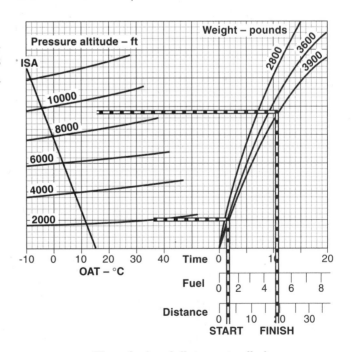

■ **Time, fuel and distance to climb**

Descent

For the descent the magnetic track is 228° with variation of 11° east. TR(M) 228, variation 11E. Therefore TR(T) 239, W/V 220/30, W/C 30 kt HEADWIND.

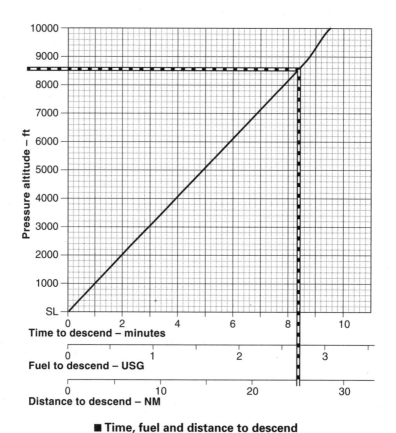

■ Time, fuel and distance to descend

	Fuel	Time	Dist
Descent from 8,500 ft to SL	3.0 USG	8.5 min	25.0 ANM
wind effect (30 kt headwind for 8.5 min)			−4.0
			= 21.0 GNM

Cruise

Total distance, Canberra to Essendon is   255.0 NM

Less: Climb   13.0

                              Descent   21.0   34.0

                    ∴ cruise distance   221.0 NM

Over the route the average track (M) of 224°, with a variation of 12° east, gives TR(T) 236, W/V (wind velocity 250°/40 knots = headwind component 40 knots).
Using our performance data of 155 kt TAS @ 17.3 USG/hr
∴ Cruise fuel   = 221 NM @ GS 115 kt (155-40) @ 17.3 USG/hr
            = 34 USG (115 min @ 17.3 rounded up from 33.25)

Flight Fuel

Climb   4.0

Cruise   34.0

Descent   3.0

∴ Total Flight Fuel   41.0 USG

Reserves

Our company policy is to always carry the recommended fixed reserve of 45 minutes endurance—45 minutes @ 20 gph = 15 USG. No variable reserve is required for a private category flight. Had this been a charter flight or IFR, then company policy requires an additional variable reserve of 15% of flight fuel.

Alternate Requirements VFR

Cloud base is 1,500 ft and the crosswind is within limits, so no alternate is required and therefore no diversion fuel.

Holding

Essendon INTER requiring 30 minutes holding fuel—30 minutes @ 20 gph = 10 USG. Also Essendon requires 10 minutes traffic holding fuel at certain times (NOTAM). This is not applicable to our planned arrival time of midday.

Taxi

Start, taxi and takeoff allowance is 3 USG.

Total Fuel Required at Start-Up

Flight fuel   41.0

Start and taxi   3.0

Fixed reserve   15.0

INTER (30-MIN)   10.0

∴ Total Fuel on Board (FOB) at start-up   69.0 USG

Weight and Balance

The basic weight of our aircraft is   2,550 lb

Pilot and passenger weight is   695 lb

Baggage weight is   187 lb

Zero fuel weight (ZFW) is   3,432 lb (which is within the 3,500 lb limit)

Fuel weight is   414 lb (69 USG @ 6.0 lb/gallon).

Ramp weight is   3,846 lb

3 gal will be burnt on start, run-up and taxi   18 lb

Takeoff weight is $\overline{3,828}$ lb

ITEM	WEIGHT	MOM/100
Basic empty weight	2550	2775
Front seat occupants	387	433
3rd & 4th occupants	308	444
Aft baggage	187	312
Zero fuel weight (3500 lbs max)	3432	3964
Fuel loading (69 gal)	414	484
Ramp weight	3846	4448
Less fuel for start, taxi and takeoff	−18	−19
Takeoff weight	3828	4429
Less fuel to destination	−240	−281
Landing weight	3588	4148

■ **BUSHCRAFT weight and balance loading form**

This takeoff weight, with the normal distribution of passengers and baggage, gives a moment of 4,429 mom/100 as shown. After a fuel burn of 240 lb, the expected landing weight is 3,588 lb. This is within the envelope as shown on the graph.

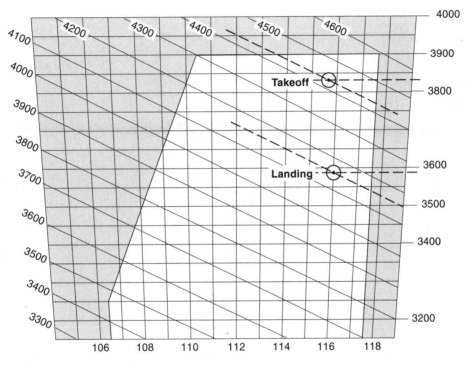

■ Gross weight/CG position at takeoff and landing

This loading is toward the aft limit of the CG range so we can expect better control response but for the same reason, reduced stability and control (higher V_{MC} if asymmetric).

Performance

Next we look at the takeoff performance. Are the runways long enough and can we clear the high terrain?

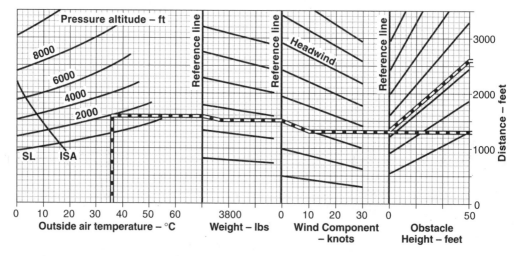

■ Takeoff distance, short, dry grass

Plotting the data for our weight and the Canberra ATIS, we have a ground roll of 1,300 ft and the distance to achieve takeoff safety speed at a height of 50 ft, is 2,600 ft. Note that we have used the chart for short, dry grass.

In Australia, it is usual to use this chart and to factor the distances by 1.15 for aircraft below 4,400 lb MTOW. This gives a ground roll of 1,495 ft and a total distance to 50 ft, of 2,990 say 3,000 ft. The reason for the factoring is to account for less than perfect performance by average and older aircraft and less than perfect conditions. It is a sensible precaution. This factoring is not obligatory but strongly recommended.

Accelerate/Stop

We now look at accelerate/stop distance:

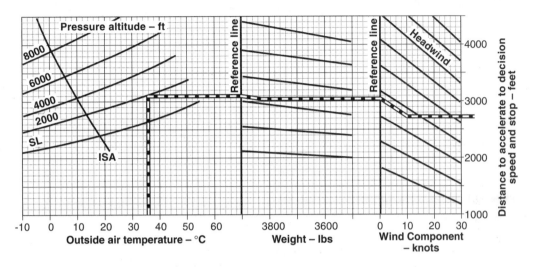

■ **Diagram of accelerate/stop distance**

The total runway distance to reach V_R of 71 kt and abort is 2,750 ft (3,200 ft factored). Therefore, the runway at Canberra will allow us to accelerate to blue line before being committed to go. Note, however, that the POH V_R is only just above V_{SO} of 70 kt. We will delay liftoff until after 75 kt but watch out for wheelbarrowing.

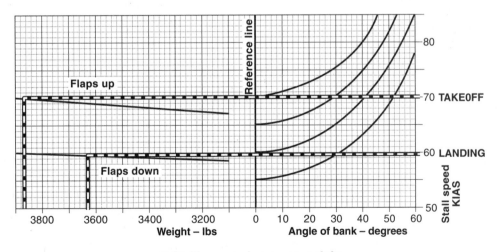

■ **Stalling speed vs gross weight**

Accelerate/Go

Some manuals include a chart for calculating when you can continue after an engine failure at liftoff. It is not a realistic option in a light twin. If the engine fails on liftoff stay on the ground. Accelerate/go is a misnomer. You are entering the *"twilight zone."*

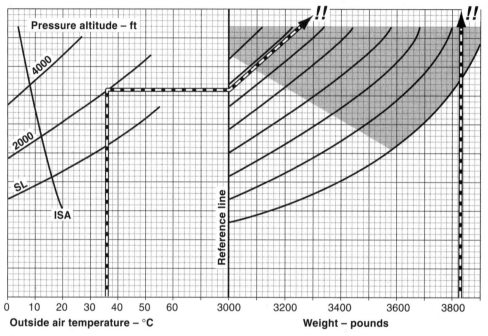

Note: 1. Ground roll distance is 20% of takeoff distance over 50-ft obstacle!
　　　2. Distances assume an engine failure at lift-off and propeller *immediately* feathered.
　　　3. Weights in shaded area may not provide positive one-engine-inoperative climb.

■ **Accelerate/Go chart**

Note that the distance to a height of 50 ft is five times the ground roll! This equates to a climb gradient of 50 ft in 5,000 ft i.e. 5 in 500 or 1.00%. This is acceptable to the regulatory authorities but you are in a *no man's land* if it happens.

Only the slightest turbulence, downdraft (common in the lee of the hills near Canberra) or delay in feathering the propeller will quickly negate any spare performance.

So, after all that, Canberra is certainly OK as far as the runway is concerned—but what about the climb gradient? There are some big hills around Canberra.

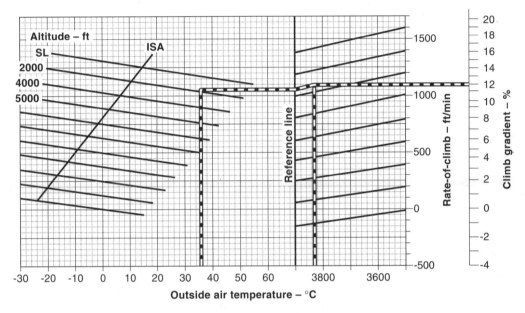

■ **Climb gradient chart—all engines operating**

Climb—All Engines Operating

Our certification requirement is that in the takeoff configuration with gear down, full power, at takeoff safety speed and out of ground effect, the aircraft must achieve a climb gradient of at least 6%. From the chart we can achieve 1,100 fpm and almost 12%. Some pilot operating handbooks show climb rates but not climb gradient. If we use the one-in-sixty rule (which is valid for small angles) then the calculation of gradient from climb rate and groundspeed, is fairly simple. As an approximate rule-of-thumb, rate of climb in fpm divided by the groundspeed in knots gives the gradient as a percentage. If the rate of climb at 70 kt was 70 fpm then the gradient would be 1%. And if the rate of climb was 210 fpm (3 × 70) the climb gradient would be 3%.

But what about the engine failure case?

We again need to know the gradient if we are considering terrain avoidance. If the chart does not show it, we can calculate it in the same way.

Let's consider two cases, engine failure after takeoff and engine failure in the cruise.

Climb—One Engine Inoperative

The POH has a second climb performance chart for the engine failed and feathered situation. The same factors of density altitude and gross weight apply.

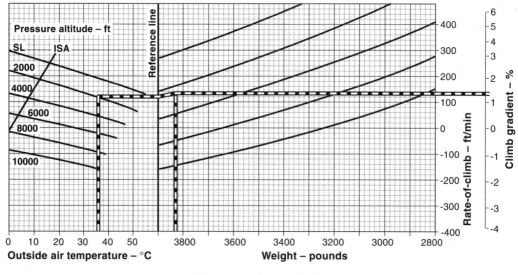

■ **Single-engine climb chart**

The chart gives a rate of climb of 140 fpm and a gradient of 1.4% at our planned takeoff weight of 3,830 lb.

Service Ceiling

Let's now consider single-engine service ceiling. LSALT for the route is 8,300 ft and the cruising level requires an even altitude plus 500.

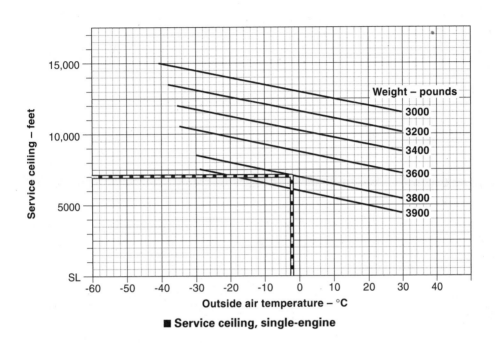

■ Service ceiling, single-engine

We can comply with both requirements at 8,500 ft. Single-engine service ceiling at 3,800 lb at a temperature (OAT) of -2°C is 7,000 ft. We could still go but we have a terrain avoidance problem and we would be staggering to avoid the high ground in the event of engine failure. We have already seen that the Albury track gives a better margin. Perhaps we should reconsider the route?

Cruise Performance

Our cruise performance is not stretched and so we can plan at recommended rather than most economical cruise. There is no need to use higher power settings unless there was a need for urgency. Today we are flying for the pleasure of it. The recommended power setting for the Bushcraft 71 gave our cruise flight fuel of 41.0 USG.

Range and Endurance

There are charts which show maximum range and endurance from full fuel but these are only of use if we are considering flights to the limit of the aircraft's capabilities. They are self explanatory.

Descent

We have previously calculated the descent but it was based on a descent rate of 1000 fpm. The chart shows that from 8,500 ft, the descent takes 8½ min, and requires 3 USG and 25 NM. However, we will plan 500 fpm for passenger comfort and we can use another rule-of-thumb. From 8,500 ft to 1,500 ft above Essendon will take 14 minutes and to calculate the distance required we simply multiply 7,000 (the altitude to be lost) × 5 = 35 nautical miles from Essendon.

Landing Performance

Our expected weight on arrival after burning flight fuel but not the fixed reserve nor holding fuel, is 3,588 lb. For our aircraft, the approach speed is 78 kt ($1.3V_{S0}$) for *all* weights. This requires a landing distance from a 50 ft height of 1,750 ft which when factored by 1.15, gives 2,070 ft, and a ground roll of 950 ft (x 1.15 = 1,093 ft). Essendon is more than adequate.

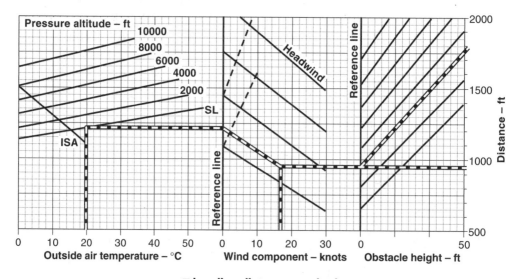

■ Landing distance required

Balked Landing (Go-Around) Performance

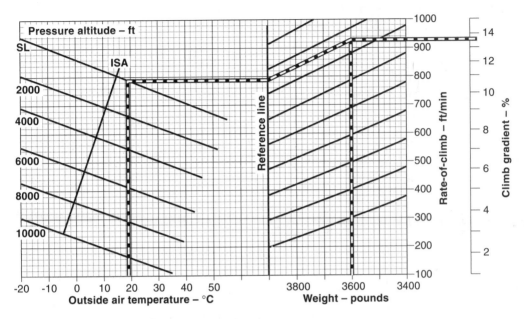

■ **Balked landing performance**

At our arrival weight of 3588 lb, the climb potential on both engines is approximately 920 fpm with a 13.5% gradient.

(Required landing climb performance by the Authority is 3.2% under ISA conditions, at or below $1.3 V_S$)

PNR and ETP

All Engines Point of No Return (PNR)

The point of no return is the last point on track where you can safely return to the point of departure (or to an alternate) with normal reserves intact. It really is a decision point for those situations where you are unable to plan to reach the destination, carry out an approach and still divert to an alternate. It is a committal point and if there is *any* doubt about the possibility of landing at the destination, the PNR is the *last* point at which you can divert. If there is doubt you must divert before this point.

To calculate the PNR for our flight from Canberra, where the alternate is the point of departure, we need to know how much fuel we would use in relation to the distance we have to travel—thus it is a function of both fuel consumption and groundspeed.

PNR Calculations (All Engines)

For an accurate PNR, we need to allow for the climb (but can ignore the descent), and ought to take into account the different cruise level for the return flight from the PNR, with the resulting differences in TAS and fuel flow. In this setting, however, the climb distance is a very small percentage of the total (13 out of 255). We can therefore ignore the climb and solve the PNR using the same TAS, wind component and fuel flow, OUT and HOME.

There are two simple methods which can be used, and both will give the same result. In both cases, the fuel available for the PNR is found as shown below. Note that the 30-minute holding fuel can be used.

	Fuel on Board (FOB) at Start-up		69.0 USG
Less:	Start & taxi	3.0	
	Fixed Reserve (FR)	15.0	18.0
	∴Flight Fuel available for PNR		51.0 USG
	TAS 155 kt	W/V 40 kt head/tail	

Method 1

Formula for distance to PNR is: $D = \dfrac{\text{Endurance} \times \text{G/S Out} \times \text{Home}}{\text{G/S Out} + \text{G/S Home (or } 2 \times \text{TAS)}}$

Endurance (51·0 USG @ 17·3 gph) = 2·95 hours

$$\therefore \text{Distance to PNR} = \frac{2 \cdot 95 \times (155 - 40) \times (155 + 40)}{115 + 195 \ (\text{or } 2 \times 155)}$$

$$= 213.4 \text{ GNM from CDB}$$

Method 2

Formula for distance to PNR is: $D = \dfrac{\text{Flight fuel available}}{\text{Rate Out} + \text{Rate Home}}$

(Note: Rate is fuel used per ground Nautical mile travelled)

Rate Out 115 kt @ 17·3 gph = 0·150 USG/GNM

Rate Out 195 kt @ 17·3 gph = 0·088 USG/GNM

∴Rate Out + Rate Home = 0·239 USG/GNM

$$\therefore \text{Distance to PNR} = \frac{51 \text{ USG}}{0 \cdot 239}$$

$$= 213 \cdot 4 \text{ GNM from CB}$$

Single-Engine PNR

For a long flight to a pinpoint destination such as an island or an airfield in the desert, it is worth also calculating the single-engine PNR. This tells us that in the event of an engine failure, we can still proceed as far as this point and make it back to the point of departure. In practice you may choose to return immediately. Conversely, if you are flying from the little island to the mainland you may wish to know how far you can proceed while waiting for the weather to lift before you have to turn back.

In our case it would be unwise to cross those mountains again on one engine, though. Let's calculate the single-engine PNR to Albury instead. However, we don't know the single-engine fuel flow and TAS.

We cannot simply halve the fuel flow as power must be increased. For this example let's assume maximum continuous on the live engine and a degraded cruise speed, a ball park figure in our case would be 11.5 gph at a TAS of 110 kt.

From the all engines operating PNR calculations, we established that we could proceed some 213 NM from CB, and still have sufficient fuel remaining to return to CB with all mandatory reserves intact. In other words, the PNR is located beyond Eildon Weir and only about 20 NM from the planned top of descent for Essendon.

For the single-engined situation, it is readily apparent that as far as abeam Albury, we will have more than adequate fuel to divert there in the event of an engine failure. However, since EN has an INTER requirement (30 minute holding) covering the period of our ETA, it would be wise to plan for a single-engine PNR based on diverting to Albury at any time after passing abeam of it.

From our En Route Chart, the distance from TOPC CB to Abeam Albury is 103 NM, and we can therefore calculate the planned fuel at that point. From this amount, we can determine the fuel available for the PNR.

For the normal cruise at 8,500 ft to the PNR we can use the forecast, W/V of 240/35. For the single-engine return to AY, we can assume a cruising level of 5,500 ft and an average TR(T) of 040°. For Subdivision B of Area 30, this W/V is 230/30.

Using the details from our initial fuel plan, we can derive the following:

	FOB at Takeoff from CB		66.0 USG
Less:	Climb	4.0	
	Cruise to Abeam Albury		
	(103 gnm @ 115 G/S @ 17.3 gph)	15.5	
	Fixed Reserve (FR) ~ 45-minutes	15.0	34.5
	∴ Flight Fuel available for PNR from ABM AY		31.5 USG

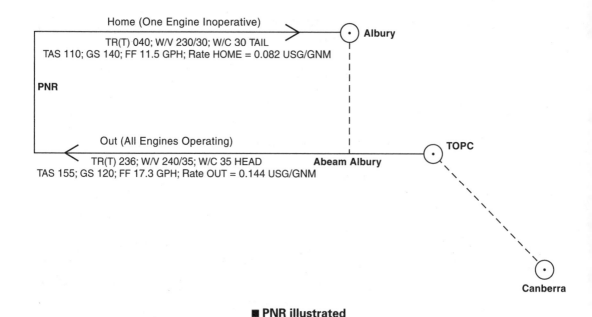

■ PNR illustrated

$$\text{Distance to PNR} = \frac{\text{Flight fuel available}}{\text{Rate Out + Rate Home}}$$

$$= \frac{31 \cdot 5}{(0 \cdot 144 + 0 \cdot 082)}$$

$$= 139 \cdot 38 \text{ (say 139) from abeam Albury}$$

The PNR is therefore just the other side of our destination, Essendon, and we will be able to divert to Albury following an engine failure at any stage after passing abeam of Albury. A good position to be in—*yes?*

Equal Time Point (ETP) or Critical Point (CP)

Of less common use is the equal time point (ETP), sometimes called critical point (CP). This is the point on track where it takes the same *time* to complete the flight to the destination as it would to return to the point of departure. It is only of significance if you have to land in a hurry say for a sick passenger or unexpected nativity. Before the ETP, it is quicker to return. After the ETP, it is quicker to continue. You can of course divert to a nearer airfield if needed—hence its limited use.

To calculate our ETP use:

$$\text{Distance to ETP} = \frac{\text{Total Distance} \times \text{G/S Home}}{\text{G/S Out} + \text{G/S Home}}$$

$$= \frac{225 \times 195}{115 + 195}$$

$$= 160 \text{ nm down track}$$

IFR Considerations

When flight planning IFR we add customarily 15% variable fuel reserve over and above the fixed reserve. Fuel policy will be contained in your company operations manual.

For this particular sector at this time of year the cruise segment is relatively safe. Airframe icing certainly becomes a concern in winter and carburetor icing can be encountered at any time.

The most important consideration for IFR planning is your escape routes.

Takeoff

Takeoff into a low cloud base (ceiling) rain, fog, reduced visibility or unclear horizon, especially in the presence of high terrain, carries risks in a light twin. Our scenario is spring/summer in Canberra but think about the consequences of engine failure after takeoff, IMC. Canberrra is almost surrounded by high terrain, especially south and west. But let's begin at the beginning. The surface wind at Canberra tends to favor Runway 30 and it is closest to our outbound track, but it's slightly shorter than 35 and has Mount Ainslie at the upwind end. Common sense suggests we should use runway 35 especially for an IFR departure.

Engine Failure Before Entering Cloud

Engine failure with a clear horizon and a defined cloud base is no different from the VFR case, although it is essential to remain clear of cloud, rain and high terrain.

We have an escape plan which here would be to continue north and turn right for downwind or even a gentle dumb-bell turn to land on RW 17. (The downwind component is only 10 kt and the runway is 9,000 ft long.)

Engine Failure After Penetrating Cloud

Now we have real problems. Picture the high terrain. Imagine the flightpath. Ask for help. Do everything carefully. Don't rush. The situation is quite controllable. Remember your training.

Climb

Climb is a worse situation for engine failure as we would have entered cloud, departed via the standard departure, which requires a 6.6% climb gradient by passing over the Brindabella mountains and have to cope with an engine failure which in this case requires an immediate turn back in cloud with all of the control, performance and system limitations that we have previously discussed.

Cruise

The single-engine service ceiling is 7,000 ft and we are over terrain which requires a LSALT of 8,300 ft. If we were IMC at 8,500 ft and one engine failed? Not pleasant to contemplate is it—descending in cloud on full power over tiger country? The route via Albury is much more attractive.

Approach and Landing

Having cleared the high terrain we are relatively safe even with a failed engine. The aircraft is lighter, we can reach Albury even if Essendon closes, and we have altitude in hand.

Conclusion

Could we have done better? Yes. We probably should have planned via overhead Albury. It's longer but all of our bases would be covered. We're clear of high terrain, less problem with engine failure, better weather, and less chance of icing. We would have an escape route from any situation. It is only 6 NM further and would cost an additional 1 USG of fuel and take 2½ minutes longer. Not a large insurance premium to stack the odds in our favor.

Chapter 7

Night Operations

Introduction

Night flying is one of the most pleasant phases of flight and is especially enjoyable in a twin. Even though the engine in a single doesn't know it's night-time, it does seem to have more vibrations, noises, fluctuations and missed beats at night (or over water, mountains or hostile terrain). The twin brings peace of mind. Of all types of flying though, night flying is only pleasant and safe if you are current (fly regularly and have flown recently) in that aircraft from that airfield. Unlike instrument flying, it cannot be practiced on your PC.

Preflight Preparation

Flight Notification

Some airports have restrictions on pattern direction at night and some runways are not available for night operations. Your instructor will explain all of these aspects in the preflight briefing.

At country airports you may need to prearrange runway and taxiway lighting if there in no pilot activated lighting (PAL) system.

Radio Procedures

There is a high cockpit workload during night pattern operations. It helps considerably if you prepare by rehearsing and memorizing all of the radio calls that will be required. These vary according to the local airport procedures. Some airports become uncontrolled after a certain time at night and you will need to be familiar with differences in radio procedures and the change in responsibility for traffic separation and spacing.

Personal Preparation

Before you go night flying, complete some day-time takeoffs and landings that day if possible in the same aircraft that you will be using for your night training. Refresh the attitude and power settings that you use during takeoff, climb, climbing turn, straight and level, level turn, descent and approach with flap. Be sure that you are really up-to-speed on checks, airspeeds, and cockpit controls. Become very familiar with the lighting controls and their operation.

It helps to practice patterns in your mind in the hangar. Memorize the checks that have to be performed in the air.

You can also minimize reflections in the cockpit windows and on the face of the instruments if you wear dark clothing rather than the traditional white shirt.

Physiological Aspects of Night Flight

The long briefing will include a refreshment of the physiological factors which affect night flying. They include:

- night vision—including dark adaptation, rods and cones and blind spots;
- space myopia—the eyes relax to focus about a meter ahead when they don't have something to focus on;
- autokinesis—apparent movement of single lights;
- somatogravic illusion (false climb); and
- leans—especially of the head is moved in two planes e.g. if you look over your shoulder when rolling into a turn. Be wary of the turn onto crosswind. Don't be in a hurry to look back at the runway. Wait until the wings are level.

Preflight Inspection of the Aircraft

Preflight inspection at night is limited by light levels on your tarmac. If you can inspect the aircraft during daytime it is better and it is preferable to use the same aircraft that you have flown that day. Conduct the normal preflight inspection including all lighting and check in particular, the serviceability of those instruments and lights required for night flying.

Especially check the cleanliness of all windows. Night vision is already limited and is particularly affected by dust and scratches on the windscreen.

Conduct the preflight inspection using a separate flashlight. Retain the full battery charge in your personal flashlight for the actual flight.

Survey the area in which the aircraft is parked. If it is on grass, unlit, near tie-down cables or amongst other aircraft, you may be able to re-position it to a paved surface with tarmac lighting and wide access. All of these simple preparations help. Allow extra time to carry out these tasks. You mustn't be in a position where you have to rush.

Cockpit Organization

Also allow extra time to settle into the cockpit and establish a comfortable lighting level. Become familiar with the location and operation of all controls and switches in this semi-darkened environment.

Keep the checklist where it is readily accessible but it is strongly recommended that you memorize all checks.

Connect your headset and adjust the intercom. Do not use a hand-held microphone for night or instrument flying unless you have no choice.

Have your flashlight very close at hand. If you need it, you will need it *right then!* Some pilots who fly regularly at night, include a Velcro patch on their flashlight and headset so that they can fly hands-free if the occasion arises.

Engine Starting

Before starting the engine, establish that the area is clear and turn on the navigation lights as a warning that you are about to start the engines.

Taxiing at Night

After start, ensure that the alternators are charging and turn on the taxi light. It is good practice to leave the strobe lights off until you reach the holding point as they can be very annoying to other crews and in conditions of mist or light rain, you will notice reflections which can be very distracting and can interfere with your visibility.

Taxi normally but with extra caution. Taxi speed should be a normal walking pace until you are clear of the parking area and on the open taxiway. Don't conduct cockpit checks until the open taxiway and then only do the essential instrument checks.

Park the aircraft in the run-up area and complete the run-up checks and pre-takeoff vital actions. Be careful of movement during run-up as it is harder to notice. Now that you are clear of tarmac lights and closer to the lighting level near the runway, re-adjust the cockpit lighting. Say the safety brief aloud—even when you are alone.

Taxi to the holding point and if you have a single taxi and landing light avoid pointing it towards landing aircraft. Check the windsock and anticipate its effect on your takeoff and pattern. Take some time here (the ten second think) to consider the effect throughout the pattern of different wind directions and speeds and the allowance you will need to make as a result. Wind at pattern altitude will be stronger than on the surface.

Stop at the holding point and turn on the strobes and transponder. Turn and leave on the pitot heat for all night flying operations. After you have takeoff clearance, line up, turn on the landing light and turn off the taxi light. Do not be in a hurry to roll. If necessary, ask for thirty seconds on the threshold when you call "ready," so that the controller knows you need the time to prepare for the takeoff.

Night Takeoff

The night takeoff is initially the same as a day-time takeoff. You will pick a point at the center of the far end of the runway as a reference for keeping straight. In this case, it will be a black hole centered between the converging rows of runway side lights. You may be able to see the red runway end lights at the far end of the runway.

Rehearse in your mind the complete takeoff until you are airborne, climbing and established in the climb attitude with landing gear and flaps up and climb power set. Remind yourself of the takeoff and climb attitude and consider your actions in the event of a need to abort the takeoff. Run up to half power on the brakes, check the engine response and roll.

Concentrate on keeping the aircraft straight as you apply full power, listen to the engine note, feel the acceleration and check the RPM and manifold pressure. Look at the black hole, check airspeed is registering and increasing—and look back at the hole.

At rotate speed, apply sufficient back pressure to raise the nose to the initial climb attitude and hold it steady, concentrating on keeping the wings level. As the wheels leave the ground, focus on the attitude indicator and the heading indicator to show any yaw. There may be some turbulence and some glare from the landing light.

Also remember the possible feeling of slowly pitching upwards (somatogravic illusion). Don't relax. You are in *no person's land*. Maintain attitude and wait. Scan the instruments until you see a positive indication of climb from the VSI and the altimeter. Airspeed should now be V_{YSE}.

Retract the gear, place your hand across the back of the power levers and maintain the attitude. You are now committed to go. Approaching 500 feet AGL, adjust the power to the climb setting, check the airspeed and readjust the attitude. Re-trim the aircraft. (If you can reach and select the landing gear and approximately adjust the power without looking inside the cockpit, other than for a brief check, then your night and instrument takeoffs will be smoother, safer and more accurate.)

Common errors are:
- to let the aircraft bank slightly during the after-takeoff checks, so it is no longer aligned with the runway;
- to lower the nose while maintaining visual contact with the runway; or
- to relax back pressure on the control column as the power is reduced and thus allow the attitude to decrease and the aircraft to settle into a reduced climb or even a shallow descent.

Night Patterns

Continue the initial climb to 500 ft AGL, look for aircraft that may be joining crosswind and commence a normal climbing turn, *on instruments*. Leave the boost (fuel) pumps on for all night patterns unless advised otherwise by the flight manual. When established crosswind, slowly look back at the runway to orient yourself and to see the general picture. To look back any earlier is risky because you have to turn further to see the runway, it is more difficult to maintain a constant attitude as you do so and you risk the leans.

Don't move your head quickly especially if you are rolling into or out of the turn, as the combined motion can induce powerful illusions.

Return to instruments to roll out straight on crosswind with some estimated, allowance for wind. Use the heading needle as a guide—it will be pointing at the right wing for a left pattern.

Remember that the aircraft is *flown* with reference to the instruments and *positioned* with respect to the runway. Only on final approach and during the initial takeoff run, is the aircraft *flown* visually.

With allowance for turn radius, the turn to downwind is initiated and the bank angle adjusted to roll out at normal lateral spacing from the runway (with the wingtip tracking down the runway).

Again use the heading needle as a guide. Thus there is a need to scan the instruments for attitude and performance, watch the runway to assess spacing, adjust the bank attitude accordingly and look for other pattern traffic. There is a tendency to think you are closer than you should be and to overcorrect.

Complete the downwind or pre-landing checks and you will see here in particular, the value of not having to read a checklist. Hold the checklist until you have three greens.

Start the stopwatch abeam the threshold and at 30 seconds (when the aircraft is on a line 45° from the runway centerline), turn base.

Initiate the base turn as you would during the day but fly with reference to the attitude indicator. Simply adjust the power, set the attitude in bank and pitch, lower the flap if appropriate, adjust the attitude and trim the aircraft. There is a need to scan from the attitude indicator to the performance instruments, to the runway and back again—similar to the downwind turn. It is a selective radial scan as you were taught in instrument flying but is widened to encompass the runway aspect. Be careful not to let the nose drop as the power is reduced.

When the attitude, power and configuration is set, accurately trim the aircraft.

Adjust the power to correct for any feeling of being too high or too low and for any expected headwind on final. Make an associated adjustment to the attitude to maintain airspeed.

Turn from base to final early.

Final Approach

Now your references and techniques change. Your scan is primarily focussed on the aspect of the runway for altitude, centerline and attitude. When the decision is made to commit to the approach, the aircraft is configured with landing flap, propellers full fine, *landing light on* and landing gear three greens confirmed.

The aircraft is trimmed and will maintain a stabilized approach. Speed should be V_{REF} (aim for a tolerance of plus 5 kt minus *nothing*).

The runway aspect will change as you get closer. It does not stay constant even on a constant approach path. The only constant is the distance of the threshold (aim point) below the horizon.

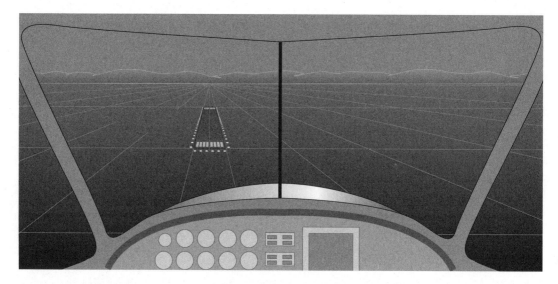

■ **Final approach—dusk**

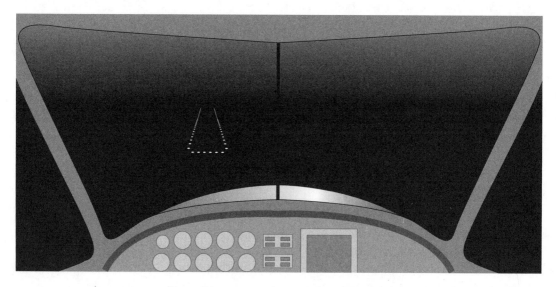

■ **Runway aspect—three degree glideslope**

At night you may not have a visual horizon but you can still picture the distance of the threshold below the horizon by imagining the point at which the runway lights converge. This is the horizon.

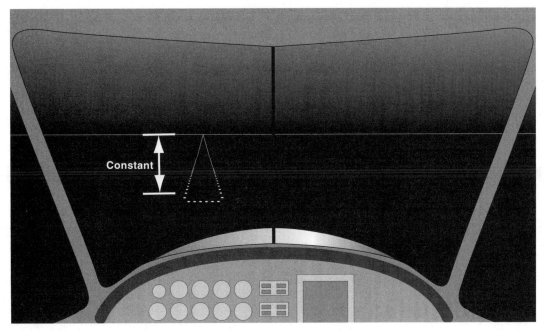

■ **The runway edges converge at the horizon**

The aspect is subtle but you will find that with practice, you will instinctively feel that you are high or low or getting that way. The significant start point is the distance of the threshold below the horizon. And it is that position which will become the important aspect of your approach judgement. It is vital to reinforce this judgement by flying fairly frequently so that it becomes a repeatable performance.

When you feel that the approach is correct you can now refine the approach by selecting a specific aim point and I would suggest a point 200 ft in from the threshold which corresponds to the central space between the first pair of white side lights as shown.

The aim point is where your eyes would impact the runway if you didn't flare. Continue the final approach now making continuous small adjustments.

Don't forget the aircraft is equipped with a rudder which is most effective in assisting lateral corrections on final. Use it in a coordinated way with aileron inputs to point the nose.

Landing

Continue to the threshold. At this point, don't look at the runway illuminated by the landing light but transfer your gaze to the *center of the far end of the runway,* gently raise the nose of the aircraft until the flightpath changes towards this point, straighten the aircraft with rudder using aileron to prevent any bank and reduce the power. As you reduce the power, maintain back pressure on the control column as if you were trying to actually reach the far end of the runway. Lower the wing to prevent drift. The aircraft will land itself.

Touch-and-go Landing

For a touch-and-go you can reselect the flap after touchdown to the takeoff setting (up) and reapply power. Be careful when retracting the flap as it is possible in some aircraft to inadvertently select the landing gear—especially at night. You may need to retrim. Be careful not to be looking inside the cockpit for too long. Try to feel and reach the controls and only look as a quick check. For retrimming it is valuable to practice and to remember how long for electric trim or how much wheel movement to approximately reset the trim from landing to takeoff. Reintroduce full power, be careful to balance the power levers and to keep straight as you do so. Keep heading for the hole at the other end of the runway. Continue for a normal takeoff, rotate and focus on the attitude indicator, watch the heading indicator and be ready for an engine failure.

Chapter 8

IFR Operations

Introduction

It is assumed that you have a current Instrument Rating/Single-Engine before embarking on twin IFR operations. If you are a little rusty, I would suggest that you reread the *Instrument Flying* manual (ASA Pilot's Manual series, ASA-PM-3). This chapter will highlight some of the considerations when operating a twin under IFR.

Preflight Preparation

The two questions that a pilot has to ask before an IFR flight are:
- Am I fit, current and prepared?
- Does the aircraft comply with IFR requirements?

Before flying a twin IFR, you need to be very comfortable with the cockpit layout, systems operation and handling characteristics of your aircraft.

Instrument flying is all about attitude and power. You *must* know the settings for your aircraft.

Preflight Planning

We discussed the planning provisions for IFR climb gradients and variable fuel reserves in the earlier chapter. Now let's consider IFR operations of our twin. The most important aspect is the takeoff planning and safety brief. If we are to takeoff into a low cloud base then we need to anticipate our options in the event of engine failure.

Normal Operations—IFR

Takeoff Brief

If you have come from a fixed gear, IFR training airplane then the step to a twin is a big one because of the performance increase, and the added complexity. Now that we have flown the twin under VFR conditions, we can look into IFR operations. The workload in a single-pilot IFR twin is the highest in pilot-land. If you can manage this and be professional about it, you are a pilot and a half.

The secret lies in the planning and preparation. Have it all done and ready. Leave plenty of time. Get it all in one pile and expect the worst. Know the aircraft, know your outbound track and frequencies, your LSALT, areas of low terrain and which way to turn. If you are not sure about any aspect, ask, study or don't go.

Assume an engine failure after takeoff and set up the aids accordingly, i.e. one set of navaids for the DP (perhaps VOR with outbound track selected and one ADF on airfield NDB frequency) and one set for the emergency return to departure airfield (other VOR on localizor frequency with ILS track set and second ADF on the locator frequency). Set first heading on the HSI. Once established outbound and incident-free, then the second set can be selected to the next way point/navaid. This is called *leap-frogging* the aids. It works very well.

Read and display the DP but also have the approach plate open and ready just in case. A typical pre-takeoff safety self briefing, IFR, would be as follows:

"This will be a visual takeoff on runway 36. My rotate speed is 75 kt for a liftoff at 80. At that point, I will have 6,000 ft of runway remaining. I will fly the aircraft in ground effect and accelerate to V_{YSE} of 85 kt. At that speed, I will select the gear up and adjust the attitude to climb on instruments. Gear selection is my decision point. If the engine fails before that point I will close both throttles and land ahead. If I have selected the gear up and transferred to instruments, I will maintain direction and climb straight ahead to the north and stay visually clear of terrain. The wind is from the northwest but there is also high ground immediately northwest of the field. If I have entered cloud, I will maintain runway heading on climb to the lowest safe altitude and ask for radar vectors for a right hand pattern and intercept of the final approach for Runway 36."

Carry out instrument, autopilot and fuel checks.
Use pitot heat, carb heat, warm the engines, strobes may be off.

Takeoff

The visual segment of an instrument takeoff is no different to VMC. If the runway is wet it will adversely affect acceleration and in the case of an abort, there will be reduced brake effectiveness and a risk of aquaplaning. Turn on the pitot heat before takeoff.

If there is rain or drizzle, it may be preferable to leave the strobe lights off as they are likely to be distracting.

Transition to instruments only when you are committed to go and have selected gear up. If you can remain visual until established in a normal climb, do so.

Climb in IMC

The higher performance of the twin makes it even more important to fly with precise reference to the attitude indicator. It significantly reduces workload and gains the optimum performance from the aircraft.

Adjust the MP in the climb and be *en garde* for carburetor icing.

We have discussed the DP from Canberra. For any IMC climb, keep in mind the high terrain below you in case you need to turn back and away from it. Adjust the mixtures, if required, in the climb.

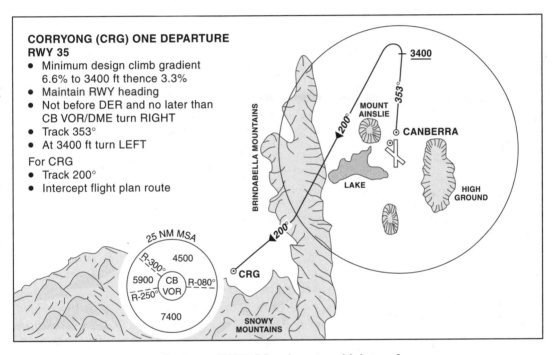

Canberra RW 35 DP—departure high terrain

141

Cruise

Establish the aircraft in the cruise and engage the autopilot if you haven't already done so. But keep an eye on it, especially monitor the attitude frequently.

Establish your normal navigation work cycle.

Descent

Before descent, confirm the weather conditions for your approach, the duty runway and the type of approach you will carry out. Organize the documentation for the approach. Run through the pre-approach briefing—even if alone. Especially consider the missed approach procedure and MDA.

If appropriate, select windscreen demist, carburetor heat and destination level plus 500 ft on the pressurization controller. Treat the turbocharger with tender loving care (TLC) and be cautious reducing power for the descent. Manage the fuel, mixtures and cowl flaps.

Instrument Approach

An instrument approach, all engines operating is no different from your advanced single. If anything the twin will be more solid and stable when established in the approach.

Abnormal Operations—IFR

Engine Failure During Takeoff—Before Decision Speed or Point

Engine failure pre-decision point means an aborted takeoff on a possibly wet runway.

Engine Failure After Decision Before IMC

Don't enter a cloud if there is a choice and only then if clean and at V_{YSE} or more. Stay clear of terrain and join for a visual pattern—a low level pattern if necessary to stay clear of cloud. In some cases a straight climb to a safe altitude even IMC may be better than trying to maneuver near the ground.

You may get radar assistance for a straight-in approach at an airfield with a longer runway, ILS and VASI. Delay the landing gear until you can intercept the normal glide-path and delay full flap until committed to land.

Engine Failure During an Approach

Be careful of the subtlety during an approach—especially the inbound turn/outside engine. There is a preference by some instructors to use the wings-level method under IFR so that the attitude indicator and skid ball always show what you are used to seeing. The small performance penalty for other than the takeoff case, is accepted. If you get confused, center the ball with rudder and either level the wings or set the desired bank angle. Hold the attitude until your body believes your eyes.

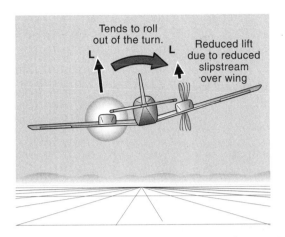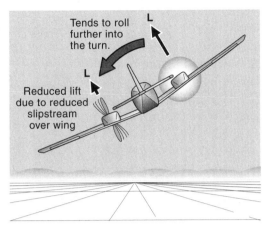

■ Engine failure during a gentle turn

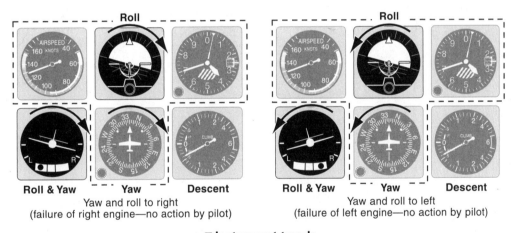

| Roll & Yaw | Yaw | Descent | Roll & Yaw | Yaw | Descent |

Yaw and roll to right
(failure of right engine—no action by pilot)

Yaw and roll to left
(failure of left engine—no action by pilot)

■ Instrument trends

How do you know the engine has failed? Yaw, roll and reduced performance obviously. But the engine instruments can be deceiving. Discuss this with your instructor. In our Bushcraft the RPM decays slowly (unless it is an engine seizure) and the MP settles around 20–22 inches. The temperatures (EGT, CHT and oil temp) all drop—EGT quite quickly. If oil pressure is lost the propeller will automatically go to full coarse but feathering must be initiated before the RPM drops below 900ish.

With an engine failure other than after takeoff, selecting full power can cause as many problems as it solves. This is especially so when IMC. What power to set on the live engine? Set the next one up, i.e. in the teardrop approach, set cruise power if clean, on ILS final set maximum continuous power, if the gear is down set full power, and if full flap has been selected, you are visual and are committed to landing anyway—aren't you? The main objective is to maintain airspeed and of course, to simultaneously keep the rate of descent under control.

Vacuum Failure

Fortunately the twin has twin vacuum pumps and so the likelihood of a total vacuum failure is remote indeed.

Flight on Partial Panel

IFR flight on partial panel is the same as the single but be wary of the performance increase when the nose is lowered.

Unusual Attitude Recovery

The loss of control situation in a twin requires prompt response. The airspeed must be kept under control. Follow the standard recovery techniques that you have been taught but also be prepared to lower the landing gear if the airspeed is getting away.

Chapter 9

Commercial Operations

Introduction

There are many factors which may make operations of your twin more complex and potentially more hazardous. As well as aspects relating to the aircraft there are other factors that you need to think about. Having mastered the aircraft you will now be embarking on flights further afield and without direct supervision. The onus is on you (whether private or commercial) to take responsibility for the way you will operate your aircraft. Your standards are ultimately your own and while some pilots will operate under an umbrella of close supervision, many will be left entirely to their own devices—as long as they get the job done, on time and within cost. The first major responsibility is your passengers.

Passengers (Private or Commercial)

This is your introduction to the twin and when you have your rating, you will be able to broaden your horizons. You will carry passengers and when you do, you have a formal responsibility to them, whether they are paying or not. An important aspect is the briefing.

The Passenger Briefing

Some will be apprehensive about flying. As well as the safety content of the briefing you do need to reassure them. This is a typical list of contents:

Before Boarding. Prior to departing the terminal building for the aircraft, brief the passengers on the following basic items:
- checking their baggage and removing potentially hazardous goods;
- carrying a lunch pack and drink with them in the cabin if they think they will need nourishment in flight;
- visiting the toilet now, rather than discover the need in flight;
- advising of any colds, flu, blocked ears or medication;
- staying together as on the walk towards the aircraft;
- not smoking on the tarmac area or in the aircraft (and perhaps anywhere in the terminal);
- keeping a watchful eye out for other aircraft, refuelling trucks, and other vehicles— especially at night or during inclement weather;
- not approaching an aircraft with an operating engine or with any lights on;
- not touching any controls unless asked; and
- obeying your instructions.

Before Starting Engines. When the preflight inspection is completed (complete it before they walk out to the aircraft if you can), strap them in and brief them on the use of their seat belts, and on any relevant emergency procedures.

A typical briefing could include:
- seat and seat belts
- smoking
- fire extinguisher
- first aid kit
- life jackets
- oxygen
- emergency exits
- doors, windows and ventilation
- radio
- planned route

Example Briefing. The briefing must be concise but cover essential safety points for the flight. Do not get really serious and frighten your passengers—remember you want them to come back and fly with you again. Be a calm, relaxed unhurried professional. Build trust.

So, how to go about it. Remember our flight from Canberra to Melbourne. Let's look at that trip:

Good morning. Welcome aboard your flight to Essendon. There are safety features built into the airplane that I would like you to be aware of.
- *Seat belts—just like your car, they must be on throughout the flight unless I tell you otherwise.*
- *The exits from the airplane are the main doors (point) and the overwing/or rear door exit. They are operated by a door catch which goes like this (demo). Only operate them if I tell you to.*
- *Lifejackets are stowed under your seat. If necessary I will tell you when to put them on and how. The seat pocket card demonstrates this.*
- *This is a no smoking flight. Government regulations apply and remember no smoking in the terminal or on the tarmac.*
- *Please enjoy your flight, if you have any questions please don't hesitate to ask me.*

Difficult Passengers

How do you cope with a contrary passenger? Tactfully, of course. Firmly, if necessary. In order of preference, you can:
- advise them;
- caution them;
- remove them;
- take them aside and explain the legal ramifications of their actions; and
- get the local law to speak to them.

If the passenger is just difficult and wants to do or go somewhere different, it helps to explain why they can't and do so in front of the other passengers. If you do it correctly you will have enlisted their aid in the cause. The other passengers may bring peer pressure to bear. Majority rules—OK?

If they won't, don't argue. Get assistance from the authorities or simply refuse to taxi the aircraft. There will always be a way (non-violent) to get the compliance of the difficult passenger.

Happy Little Vegemites

Children require special consideration and treatment. Don't always rely on the adult or parent keeping little Johnny under strict control especially on the tarmac and especially if you let the little one occupy the right hand seat. Switches have a habit of changing position and it is not unusual to have the flaps or radio frequency selected when you don't really need it.

Babies are in most ways easier but be very careful during descent. The baby can't tell you if the rate of descent is too great.

Descent Planning

All of our pre-takeoff planning, departure considerations and enroute work can be undone by a poorly planned descent. You will remember that we talked about the descent profile during the trip to Essendon. Let's look at a few basic rules of descent.

Unpressurized. Don't exceed 800 fpm in descent. Remember 500 fpm is nice, 800 is acceptable but any more and you expose yourself and your passengers to possible problems with the eardrum and blocked sinus.

Pressurized Flight. Higher altitudes offer a lovely way to fly but they do add their own planning problems. For instance, does the descent profile you have selected allow time for the cabin pressure to get to ground level?

For example, cruising at 18,000 ft, descent point 54 NM (3 × altitude), GS typically 210 kt, ETI 15½ minutes, cabin pressure 7,000 ft, the time to depressurize cabin at 500 fpm = 14 minutes. (This is obviously marginal. It would be wise to descend cabin at say 700 fpm = 10 minutes.)

Consider a higher flight: flight level 210, descent point 63 NM (3 × altitude), 18 min to reach destination, cabin pressure about 10,000 ft, therefore at 500 fpm, it will take 20 minutes to get the cabin down to sea level.

So, there is a new consideration in planning. How long it takes to reduce the cabin pressure at a comfortable rate versus how long to reach your destination. In most cases, the pressurization differential is acceptable for normal descent, but you must consider cabin altitude.

Also don't forget if you fly from Essendon to Canberra (pressurized), you need to set the altitude above the elevation of the field (Canberra) not sea level. A very important item, not remembered by a pressurized turboprop pilot who flew from Australia to Papua New Guinea one day.

His destination was the highland airport of Mount Hagen. He set sea level on the "box." Hagen is 5,000 ft AMSL. Normally, a micro-switch on the landing gear depressurizes the aircraft (ready or not) on landing—this day, it didn't.

The pilot struggled to open the door (lots of pressure inside) and when he finally succeeded, the pressure pushed the door rather rapidly outwards with a very surprised pilot still hanging onto the handle.

Not a very dignified arrival, although the native community thought it was memorable.

Crew

Crew Briefing

If you are operating in a two-pilot cockpit, you should give an operational briefing to your copilot, perhaps considering:
- Taxi route to runway.
- Takeoff procedures and route to follow.
- Action in the case of an engine failure.
- Your role/his or her role/your expectations.

Cargo

Hazardous Materials

This is a long and quite complicated subject. The best solution is to complete a HazMat course. This gives you the best available information about a complex subject.

You will be surprised at the items that comprise hazardous materials:
- What you must not carry.
- What you should not carry.
- What requires special packaging/handling.

Some time back, a 44-seat turbo-prop was on climb through 10,000 ft when the Flight Attendant opened the cockpit door to tell the flight crew of a "small problem." She reported, "there is a lot of smoke in the cabin." The Captain and First Officer both turned around to see the attendant engulfed in a cloud of billowing white "smoke." Their reaction was immediate and not unexpected:
- *emergency descent;*
- *ATC advised of problem;*
- *lots of radio calls;*
- *oxygen masks on;*
- *emergency declared;*
- *priority landing requested;*
- *straight-in approach;*
- *emergency landing;*

- *emergency evacuation of passengers and crew; and*
- *fire crews in attendance.*

The reaction of the crew (at a safe distance) when they saw the fire crew (suited up in all their glory) leaving the aircraft and laughing aloud was understandable: "What have we done?"

"Nothing," was the answer. "Someone" had loaded a consignment of animal sperm, packed in a container of dry ice (frozen carbon dioxide). They did not declare it and did not put safety latches on the pressure relief seals.

Result? The pressure plugs blew, the cabin was filled with white smoke-like vapor and the result—the emergency evacuation. The outcome could have been much much worse.

Animals

Most animals are loveable and affectionate—most of the time. However, in aviation they present a unique and complex problem in either carrying them, having them on or near the runway or meeting them in the air.

On the Runway

On the runway or close by, animals are both a distraction to the crew and a possible hazard to the aircraft. Have the animals moved away before you land or takeoff. You cannot assume they will run the other way when you apply power.

Not recommended is the action of a tropical based pilot who carried a pistol. He saw a pack of dogs on the runway who defied all attempts to chase them off. A little impatient with the clearing process, our gallant pilot opened a side window and proceeded to (try) shoot the animals—in true Wyatt Earp fashion.

- *He was a terrible shot!*
- *He missed every one of them!*
- *He cleared the runway (and most of the airfield) of fellow pilots, ground staff and engineers!*
- *He fatally wounded 4 runway lights and part of the VASI system!*
- *He was charged for the offence!*
- *The company took a very dim view of the episode (a VERY dim view).*

As Freight

Animals and pets require specialized handling.

The pet must be carried in a special container with absorbent mats, separated from passengers and usually sedated by a vet. Be careful loading and unloading them. Remember, they have been caged and put in dark holes (the baggage locker area). They may be a little "miffed" (upset). You can't really blame them if they decide to bite or scratch the nearest human (possibly you) as you move the cage. Cats in particular, get very alarmed and come out fighting.

Wear gloves. If you are scratched or bitten seek medical advice.

Native animals can also be dangerous cargo unless correctly packed.

A well known story in aviation relates to an oil rig worker returning back to the "big smoke" from his tour in the Simpson Desert gas basin. His children had queried him about the goannas and being a bright young man, he decided to catch one to show the children.

The hunt was successful, but no cage! (NB: A goanna can approach the size of a small crocodile). No problem. Get a large shoe-box and stuff the live goanna inside. Should be okay—short air trip for only 2 hours. He took the box on board the light, nine-seat twin. En route, the goanna became tired of the enforced imprisonment, broke open the box and like all goannas, headed for the tallest object to climb to safety. In this instance, it was the nearest human body.

As luck would have it, the aircraft had a divider and door between the cockpit and cabin. The pilot took one look at the goanna, executed a command decision and shut the door (fast). This isolated the goanna with the passengers. The pilot was free to do his job.

The resulting "carnage" (brawl) between passengers and goanna resulted in 30 stitches (humans), busted seats (2 of them) and a very upset goanna—which ended up in the local zoo.
We won't even consider snakes and ferrets.

Birds

Birds are a daily hazard. Don't try to out maneuver them. Remember that birds have very good eyesight and awareness. They have to, in order to survive in their world. They will see you and will dive away or turn. By trying to avoid them you introduce uncertainty and may cause the very impact you were trying to avoid.

You can help their awareness. Turn the radar on and use landing lights for takeoff climb, descent and approach. If operating low level, leave your lights on. Also slow down at lower altitudes so that they have a chance to hear you coming and to get out of your way.

Pressures
Hurry Up and Wait

The pilot's life includes extended periods of waiting and then when a task arises there is always a deadline. Hurrying is okay. Short cuts are not. The accident case studies include many avoidable, human error accidents including:

- fuel contamination (no fuel drain);
- fuel exhaustion (no fuel dip);

- engine problems (run-up while taxiing, no run-up, excessive RPM drop, no warm-up);
- control problems (rushed checks, pitot cover left on, ice not removed, seat not locked); and
- overweight (no weighing of pax or cargo, no takeoff performance calculations).

Can't Weight to get Airborne?

Don't be rushed into a hurried take off. Do all of the calculations.

Weather to Go or Stay

Many passengers will be keen to reach their destination but they do not understand the full ramifications of pressing on. Only you know the real risks involved.

Be prepared to delay—remember the forecast periods. Ask ATC or call the destination.

Leigh Creek one day had appalling forecasts. The local passengers were really "pushy"—must get back to Leigh Creek—it's Sunday. The pilot wasn't happy—a simple look out of the window of the Adelaide terminal window suggested that a warm fire and a book would be a better idea. The Leigh Creek refueller advised by telephone that any pilot who flew that day was "nuts." However, psychological pressure built. The aircraft departed, had a really rough trip, made three instrument approaches, never saw a thing and ended up at their alternate airport—guess where—Adelaide. Five hours of flying. The airport at Leigh Creek opened up some two hours after the aircraft diverted back to Adelaide. A simple delay in departure time would have given the aircraft and passengers a much better chance of getting into their destination. It also would have avoided five hours of flying, upset/sick passengers and a very tired single pilot. Not a good outcome—for anybody.

Ground Handling—Single Pilot

You will have to assist with loading and carrying baggage to and from the aircraft. Protect your back and your hearing.

Getting It Together

Duty Times and Crew Rest

Fatigue is insidious. It creeps up on you and usually manifests itself in the middle of a descent or while attempting a particularly difficult crosswind landing. The results are usually embarrassing and potentially fatal. You can go beyond feeling tired and then the situation becomes really dangerous. Coffee is not the solution. Nor is alcohol when you want to sleep. A small amount can relax you but more will not produce restful sleep and the fatigue will be carried over to the next day. Some people have the ability to take "cat-naps" between tasks, others of us have to find a quiet, cool and comfortable place. Some of us can survive for a while on six hours sleep, others need eight. Be aware of your own sleep requirements and allow for them. The rules are there for your protection and the safety of you and your passengers.

FLW's (Famous Last Words)

It's only a passing shower.
I'll make it just before dark.
There should be enough fuel to make it there and back without refuelling.
An extra 20 or 30 gallons won't make that much difference.
I've done it before and it was okay.
There's no need to drain the tanks, Jim's tanker is always immaculate.
There's no run-up area, I'll check the magnetos on takeoff.
The windscreen will clear as we accelerate.
The mag drop and rough running is just lead build-up on the plugs.
It's a fuel gauge malfunction (or any other gauge).
It was working OK yesterday.
If you delay rotation on takeoff you'll be able to climb over the trees.
The runway is long enough even at 40°C.
I'll flare over the under-run and touch down on the first brick.
The max crosswind is for student pilots.
It'll be clear on the other side of the mountains.
She'll be right (C'est la vie)!

Airmanship

Simply, airmanship is *care in the air.*
- *Care* for the aircraft, other airspace and airfield users, passengers, ground handlers, maintenance personnel, air traffic controllers, employers. Is is also care about oneself, flight planning, preflight preparation. It is about care to avoid accidents.
- *Caution* about deteriorating situations.
- *Consideration* for people.
- *Concern.*

If you care for the aircraft, your profession, other pilots, air traffic services, despatchers, passengers and ground staff, they will care for you.

Chapter 10

Multi-Engine Rating

Introduction

The course of flight and ground training described herein provides the instructor and student with a basis for the training program and follows best practice as far as educational principles and instructional techniques are concerned. Candidates should reference the Practical Test Standards for a complete description of the evaluation minimums.

Overall Objective of the Multi-Engine Rating

The objective of the course is for the candidate to have a sound theoretical knowledge of multi-engine aircraft operation and to have the skills and the right mental attitude for the safe and competent operation of such aircraft.

Course Structure

The course comprises a minimum of eight lectures and eight flight exercises which include briefings. The 8 hours of flight time should include at least 3½ hours of asymmetric training and 1 hour of instrument flying (for instrument rated pilots). The program also includes a night element.

The design of the program allows for a series of eight lectures which provide the theoretical foundation on which the flight exercises are built (e.g. What is a turbocharger? How does it work?). The long briefings then focus on the practical operation of the specific aircraft and systems under normal and abnormal operations and concentrates on procedures, pilot actions and responsibilities, (e.g. How to operate this turbocharger in this aircraft and what checks and balances are required to monitor correct operation). There is then a preflight briefing to describe the actual flight sequence that is about to be followed, (e.g. Who will be doing what and when).

The ground and flight training should be integrated and coordinated so that the candidate gains the maximum transfer of learning. The lecture should be conducted shortly (a day or two) before the relevant flight exercise. It should form the basis for a review at the beginning of the long briefing to ensure that the student comprehends what is about to be explained and then demonstrated in the air. The lectures, briefings and flight sequences include reviews and standards so that the progress of the student can be verified before moving on to the next activity. During the course of the rating, the successful completion of each sequence should be recorded.

Instructional Technique

The program is built on the principle that learning outcomes can be measured, and must be, to ascertain if the training was effective. Thus the instructor has to *transfer* knowledge, attitudes, habits and skills to the student and then measure the result. The objectives and correct information must be clearly defined in the instructor's mind before the program begins. The student will tend to do what the instructor does not so much what he or she says. As well as the verbal instruction, it is important for the instructor to set an example of professionalism.

The program is built on the sequence of:
- *explain* the principle of operation in the theory lecture;
- *describe* practical operation in the long briefing and preflight briefing;
- *demonstrate* (the instructor shows how to do it correctly) in the aircraft;
- *guide* (allow the student to try it but provide active guidance to help in achieving the task); and
- *supervise* (allow the student to operate without active instruction—to make mistakes and to make corrections—but keep an eye on it).

Ground Training

The theoretical training comprises a total of eight lectures on subjects associated with the operation of multi-engine aircraft. It provides the theoretical basis for the flight exercises and includes elements which are related to the type of airplane to be used for the rating.

The syllabus is as follows:

Lecture	Subject	Duration
LB1	Aircraft Systems	1 hr
LB2	Engine, Propeller and Fuel Systems	1 hr
LB3	Principles of Multi-Engined Flight	1 hr
LB4	Minimum Control & Safety Speed	1 hr
LB5	Effect of Engine Failure on Systems & Performance	1 hr
LB6	Weight & Balance (Loading) and Passengers	1 hr
LB7	Performance	1 hr
LB8	Flight Planning	1 hr

Before completing flying training, including the briefings, the candidates should satisfactorily complete a questionnaire on systems, limitations, procedures and performance.

Flight Training

The flight training element of the initial multi–engine course consists of eight exercises, each of which includes a long briefing, a preflight briefing and suggested flight profile. Actual flying includes a minimum of 8 hours of dual instruction including 3½ hours of asymmetric training, a one hour instrument flight and a one hour night flight. The syllabus automatically encompasses type conversion training for the airplane used on the course.

The outline syllabus is as follows:

Exercise	Description	Flight Duration
F1	Introduction to Type	1 hr
F2	General Handling & Patterns	1 hr
F3	Introduction to Asymmetric Flight	1 hr
F4	Critical & Safety Speeds	1 hr
F5	Asymmetric Patterns	1 hr
F6	Asymmetric Performance & Patterns	1 hr
F7	Instrument Flying	1 hr
F8	Night Patterns	1 hr

On successful completion of the training program, the candidate will undergo a final assessment flight with an Designated Pilot Examiner or an FAA Examiner.

If the candidate does not hold an instrument rating, exercise F7 should be omitted; however, the balance of flight hours should remain unchanged.

On completion of the training, the candidate should be capable of handling the airplane safely and confidently under both the normal and asymmetric condition. Essential (minimum) and desirable standards are described in each flight profile. If the student does not achieve the objectives or reach the standard, the briefing or flight must be repeated.

Lecture: L1—Aircraft Systems

Objectives

At the end of the lecture the student should be able to describe the systems of the aircraft and specify any limitations relevant to their operation.

Lecture Content

Aircraft Systems (Normal and Abnormal Operation)

- **Electrical.** Describe the system and services provided under normal and abnormal operations. Especially cover services that must be load-shed in the event of a failure of a particular engine or alternator. It is important that the student be able to recall actions required VFR, Night and IFR to conserve electrical power for a safe flight completion.
- **Primary and secondary flight controls.** The primary flight controls, trim and flap systems should be described including normal functioning and limitations.
- **Hydraulics, landing gear and brakes.** The description of the landing gear and associated electrohydraulic system should cover normal operation and indications and the manual extension methods. The relationship between electrics and hydraulics should be covered and the different reversionary modes available to the pilot. Associated indications should be included. Discuss also the squat switch, warning horn and its relationship with the throttle position, flap position and airspeed. Caution against cancelling the warning horn. The student should be able to describe the systems and functions and correctly state manual operation.
- **Flight instruments.** Any unusual or more complex instruments such as digital or multi-function displays should be covered in detail. Especially discuss any ergonomic problems associated with the instruments or their position. Highlight what would be lost with vacuum or electrical failures.
- **Avionics and autopilot.** Encourage use of the autopilot to reduce workload and develop confidence by describing the various functions, their advantages and also disconnect options. While describing the autopilot also highlight the need to monitor its functions especially during flightpath changes.
- **De-icing, anti-Icing and de-misting.** All systems should be described as well as the need for anticipation to avoid major icing or misting problems. Reemphasize the symptoms of pitot, induction and carburetor icing and how to avoid it.
- **Oxygen.** The oxygen system must be stressed as a life support system and the immediate actions in the event of cabin decompression should be rehearsed until almost automatic. The student should be able to correctly describe the immediate actions without hesitation. Discuss the effects and symptoms of hypoxia. Discuss the methods and dangers associated with emergency descent.
- **Cabin heating, air conditioning and pressurization.** As well as describing the systems and their functions, stress the effect of engine failure on these systems. The importance of monitoring pressurization schedules during climb and descent should be stressed.

Lecture: L2—Engines, Propeller and Fuel Systems

Learning Objectives

At the end of the lecture the student should be able to correctly describe the engines and their related systems. The correct techniques for power adjustments and precautions to be taken with the turbocharger should be clear—together with the operation of the feathering mechanism. Whenever discussing systems particularly explain the symptoms, diagnosis and correct actions in the event of unusual or unexpected responses to control inputs, i.e. what can go wrong, what can you accept and what can you do about it.

Lecture Content

Engine Systems (Normal and Abnormal Operation)

- **Engine controls.** Fuel feed, fuel injection, boost pumps, mixture control, carburetor heat, cowl flaps and their correct operation should be stressed. Turbocharger principles and operation must be stressed.
- **Propellers.** Propeller operation, governed and ungoverned, feathering and unfeathering, RPM synchronization and loss of oil pressure must be discussed. The relationship between forces acting on the propeller and the role of oil pressure, the unfeathering accumulator and the anti-feathering latch mechanism should be discussed.
- **Fuel.** Particularly emphasize the fuel distribution, the automatic and manual selections, crossfeed and any need to transfer fuel. The fuel indicating system should be described and any limitations or known ergonomic problems with fuel system operation should be highlighted. The student must be able to recall fuel quantities, type, any required transfer sequence and crossfeed operation. Fuel drains should be identified.
- **Oil.** Minimum oil quantities, oil types, inspection, and refill points should be described.
- **Starter.** The starter system, engine priming, internal and external power starts, starter limitations, hot starts, cold starts and emergencies on start must be covered in detail. Started limits must be recalled correctly. Airstart techniques, though only to be used by the student in exceptional circumstances, should be described.
- **Ignition.** Symptoms of ignition problems on run-up and means of diagnosing and perhaps correcting them, should be covered. Differences in symptoms between magneto and injector faults should be discussed.

Lecture: L3—Principles of Multi-Engine Flight

Learning Objectives

At the end of the lecture, the candidate should have a sound knowledge of the aerodynamic principles involved in multi-engine flight in normal and asymmetric conditions and be able to state the primary forces and moments acting on the aircraft and the different means of control.

Lecture Content

- **Review.** Angle of attack, sideslip angle, yaw and balance and the major forces and moments acting on the aircraft.
- **Multi-engine environment.** Rationale for 2 or more engines and configurations of multi-engine airplanes.
- **Multi-engine problems.** Engine failure leading to control difficulties and performance reduction.
- **Aerodynamics of asymmetry.** Cover the following forces and conditions.
  - Thrust (yawing moment):
    - asymmetric blade effect;
    - torque reaction.
  - Drag:
    - failed engine drag (offset drag line);
    - total drag.
  - Lift:
    - asymmetry (slipstream effect).
  - Dynamics of failure:
    - effect of yaw;
    - sideslip/sideforces;
    - thrust/drag.
  - Controllability in asymmetric flight:
    - rudder, aileron and elevator;
    - balanced/unbalanced flight (effect of bank/sideslip);
    - fin strength, and stall;
    - trimming.

Lecture: L4—Minimum Control and Safety Speeds

Learning Objectives

At the end of the lesson the student must have a full understanding of the principles involved in, and the factors affecting, minimum control and safety speeds. The student will be able to state the actual speeds for the aircraft type and the relationship with stalling speed.

Lecture Content

- **Minimum control speed.**
  - Definition.
  - Derivation.
  - Factors affecting:
    - thrust and power;
    - weight/CG;
    - altitude;
    - drag (e.g. landing gear, flaps, feathering);
    - turbulence;
    - critical engine (if applicable);
    - P factor.
- **Pilot actions.**
  - Sequence.
  - Skill/strength.
  - Reaction time.
  - Effect of bank.
- V_{MC}.
- V_S.
- **Takeoff safety speed (TOSS or V_2).**
  - Definition.
  - Derivation.
- V_X, V_{XSE}, V_Y, V_{YSE} **(Blue Line).**
- **Summary.** The importance of airspeed and the methods and sequence for regaining control following engine failure.
- **Discussion.** The concept of decision speed and point for takeoff and decision height for landing.

Lecture: L5—Effects of Engine Failure on Systems and Performance

Learning Objectives

At the end of the lesson the candidate will be able to state the effects on systems and aircraft performance in flight caused by one engine being inoperative.

Lesson Content

- **Effect on systems.**
  - Electrics.
  - Hydraulic.
  - Fuel.
  - Air conditioning and pressurization.
  - Instruments and navaids.
  - Autopilot.
  - Others (type related).
- **Effect on thrust and power.**
  - Excess thrust available.
  - Excess power available.
  - Optimum speeds (V_{XSE}, V_{YSE}).
- **Effects on takeoff performance.**
- **Derivation of decision speeds and points.**
- **Rejected takeoff.**
- **Effect on cruise performance.**
  - Service ceiling.
  - Range.
  - Endurance.
- **Effects on landing and go-around performance.**
- **Effects on the pilot.** Sensations of engine failure.

Lecture: L6—Weight and Balance (Loading)

Learning Objectives

At the end of the lesson, the candidate will be able to correctly complete the weight and balance calculations for the aircraft type for a typical range of loadings and give a demonstration passenger briefing.

Lecture Content

- **Conversion.** U.S. and metric units (if applicable to your operation).
- **Revision.** Weight and balance principles.
- **Emphasis.** The effects on control and performance of loading outside of weight and balance limits.
- **Standard passenger weights.** Including the limitations of their use.
- **Weight and balance calculations.** For the specific aircraft type.
- **Loading system and weight distribution.**
- **Cargo.** Cargo versus fuel and the trade-off options.
- **Securing cargo.**
- **Hazardous materials.** An introduction to the more common hazardous materials.
- **Carriage of animals.**
- **Carriage of passengers.** Provisions, restraint and emergencies.
- **Passenger occupying the right hand seat.** Regulations and precautions.
- **Care of passengers.** On the tarmac and in flight.
- **The passenger briefing.**

Lecture L7—Performance

Learning Objectives

At the end of the lesson the candidate will be able to correctly calculate aircraft climb, descent, cruise, takeoff and landing performance and derive from the charts in the aircraft's flight manual, the specific parameters for the aircraft, with all engines operating and with one engine inoperative.

Lecture Content

- **Revision.** U.S. vs metric units
- **Revision.** Applicable Federal Aviation Regulations and SOPs.
- **Revision.** Principles of weight and performance calculations, use of graphs and tables.
- **Practice calculations.** For the airplane type, using flight manual data.
  - Takeoff.
  - Accelerate/stop.
  - Climb out—flightpaths.
  - Service ceiling.
  - Descent.
  - Landing.
  - Go-around.
- **Discussion.** The effect on takeoff and landing performance of water, grass, slope and unprepared surfaces.
- **Explanation.** The value of using factored takeoff distances.

Lecture: L8—Flight Planning

Learning Objectives

At the end of the lesson the candidate will be able to completely and correctly plan a cross-country flight VFR, night, or IFR (according to his or her previous experience).

Lecture Content

- **Discussion.** The company's policy with regard to fuel reserves.
- **Selection of route.**
- **Selection of cruise altitude.**
- **Selection of cruise power.**
- **Range and endurance.**
- **Holding and diversion.**
- **Alternate airfield requirements.** Night and IFR if appropriate.
- **ETP, CP and PNR.** Including single-engine.
- **Escape routes.**
- **In flight calculations.**
- **Rules of thumb.**
- **Performance.** Derivation of a performance and planning "mud map" or guide for typical weights and loadings.

Exercise F1
Introduction to Aircraft Type—Long Briefing

Objectives
At the end of the briefing the candidate will be able to correctly describe the techniques, attitudes and power settings for normal takeoff, climb, cruise and descent. He or she will correctly state the engine start and shutdown procedures.

Briefing Content
Introduction
- **Advantages and limitations of a twin.**

Considerations
- **Review.** Theory lesson including questions and clarification of any uncertainties.
- **Definitions.** Confirm understanding of definitions and terminology to be used on the flight exercise.
- **Limitations.** Introduce the V_N diagram for the specific aircraft and explain the flight envelope and the structural, control and airspeed limitations.

Application
- **Introduction.** Procedures and checks for normal operations.
- **Start procedures.**
- **Taxiing techniques.**
- **Run-up checks.** Especially crossfeed and autopilot.
- **Safety brief example.**
- **Pre-takeoff vital actions.**
- **Takeoff and climb.**
  - Checklist procedures.
  - Normal takeoff/crosswind takeoff.
  - After take-off checks.
  - Normal climb, climbing turns.
  - Engine handling.
  - Pressurization.
- **Cruise.**
  - Level off.
  - Use of cowl flaps.
  - Synchronizing the propellers.
  - Turbocharger operation.
  - Trimming.

■ **Introduction to the handling characteristics.**
- Effect of flaps, landing gear.
- Normal turns.
- Cruise checks.

■ **Engine handling.**
- Engine temperatures and pressures.
- Use of:
  - mixture control;
  - carburetor heat.

■ **Normal pattern and landing.**
- Checklist procedures.
- Approach.
- Normal landing.
- Aim point.
- Touchdown.

Conclusion (Summary and Review Questions)

Summary of main points including questions to ascertain if the learning objectives were achieved. Summary of normal attitudes, power settings and performance.

Exercise F1
Introduction to Aircraft Type—Preflight Briefing

(The words in italics indicate the instructor/student participation for each exercise.)

Aim

To familiarize the candidate with the handling characteristics of the aircraft in normal flight. At the end of the flight, the candidate should know the normal and emergency checklist procedures, and be able to handle the airplane competently. He or she should be able to taxi using differential thrust, synchronize the props, trim in all axes and set the correct attitudes and power settings for each flightpath.

Air Exercise

- **Preflight preparation and aircraft inspection.**   *demonstrate*
- **Start-up and taxiing.**
  - Cockpit familiarization.
  - Checklist procedures.   *demonstrate and guide*
  - Engine start (discuss engine fire on the ground).
  - Taxiing.   *guide*
  - Use of brakes.
  - Use of throttles.
- **Run-up and safety briefing.**   *demonstrate*
- **Takeoff and climb.**   *demonstrate*
  - Checklist procedures.
  - Normal takeoff/crosswind takeoff.
  - After takeoff checks.
  - Normal climb, climbing turns.   *guide*
  - Attitudes and power settings.
- **Cruise.**
  - Level off.
  - Use of trim.
  - Effect of flaps, landing gear.   *guide*
  - Normal turns.
  - Cruise checks.
- **Engine handling.**
  - Engine temperatures and pressures.
  - Use of:
    - mixture control;   *guide*
    - carburetor de-icing (as appropriate).

■ **Demonstration normal pattern.**   *demonstrate*
  • Checklist procedures.
  • Approach and normal landing.

Flightpath	Attitude	Power	Performance
Climb			
Fast cruise			
Slow cruise			
Cruise descent			
Approach			

Airmanship Points

■ **Lookout/the clock code.**
■ *"I have control"/"You have control."* Handing over/ taking over.

Emergencies

■ **Radio failure.**
■ **Actual engine failure.**

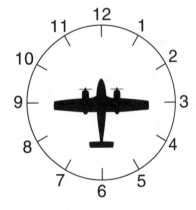

■ **The clock code**

Exercise F2
General Handling and Patterns—Long Briefing

Learning Objectives
At the end of the briefing the student will be able to describe the behavior of the particular aircraft during the stall and recovery and the correct recovery technique. He will recall the normal pattern including attitudes, power settings and configurations, checks and radio calls.

Introduction
Review of previous flight and briefing.

Considerations
- **Review.** Symptoms of the stall.
- **Stall avoidance.**
- **Stall recovery technique.**

Application
- **Stalling.**
  - Clean configuration—power off.
  - Approach configuration—power off.
  - Approach configuration—power on turning.

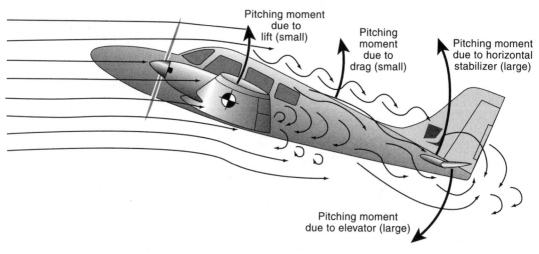

■ Stall and recovery

- **Emergency descent.**
- **Pattern procedures.** Both engines operative.

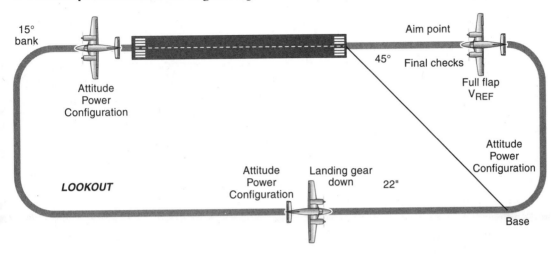

■ **Normal pattern**

- Normal pattern.
- Flapless approach and landing.
- Performance landing.
- Go-around.
- Touch and go.
- **Landing gear emergency lowering procedures.**

Conclusion (Summary and Review Questions)

Exercise F2
General Handling and Patterns—Preflight Briefing

Aim

The aim is to revise airplane and engine handling, and practice pattern procedures. At the end of the flight the student will be able to safely and correctly recover from a stall, identify and avoid an approaching stall and conduct normal patterns and landings to an acceptable standard. The candidate should demonstrate his or her ability to handle all aspects of normal aircraft operation with both engines operative.

Air Exercise

- **Start-up and taxi.**   *supervise*
- **Normal takeoff and climb.**   *supervise*
- **Stalling.**
  - Clean configuration power off.   *demonstrate, guide, supervise*
  - Approach configuration—power off.
  - Approach configuration—power on.
- **Emergency descent.**
- **Pattern procedure** (both engines operative).
  - Normal configuration.   *demonstrate, guide, supervise*
  - Flapless approach and landing.
  - Performance landing.
  - Go-around.
- **Landing gear emergency procedures.**   *guide*

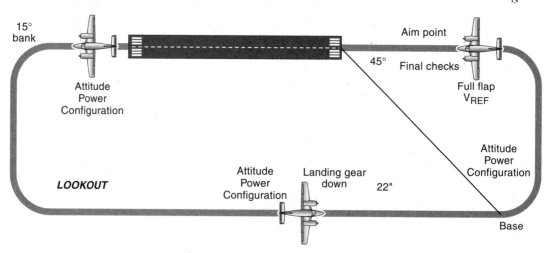

■ Normal pattern

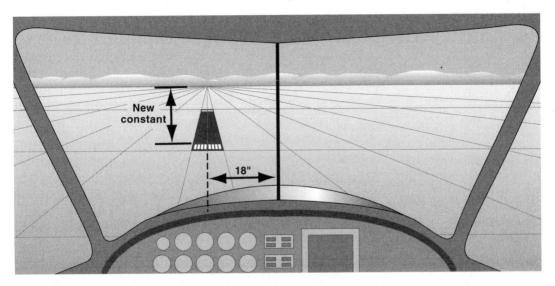

■ **Stabilized approach**

Airmanship
■ **Pre-stalling check.**

H	Height	To recover by 1,500 ft
A	Airframe	Flaps Up or Set
S	Security	Harnesses No Loose Items
E	Engine	Temps and Pressures Mixture Full Rich Carb Heat Set Fuel Pump On
L	Location	Not over water, cloud or buildings
L	Lookout	Clearing Turn

■ **Lookout.**

Emergencies
■ **Unlatched door.**
■ **Bird strike.**
■ **Wheels up landing.**
■ **Stall/spin/unusual attitude recovery.**

Exercise F3
Introduction to Asymmetric Flight—Long Briefing

Objectives

At the end of the briefing the student will be able to correctly describe the methods of control in the event of engine failure and the pros and cons of each. He will state the immediate actions and be able to provide a demonstration safety briefing.

Introduction

Review previous exercise and reinforce important elements. Stress the importance of correct response to engine failure and the need to practice on the ground.

Considerations

■ **Review of previous flight and lessons.**

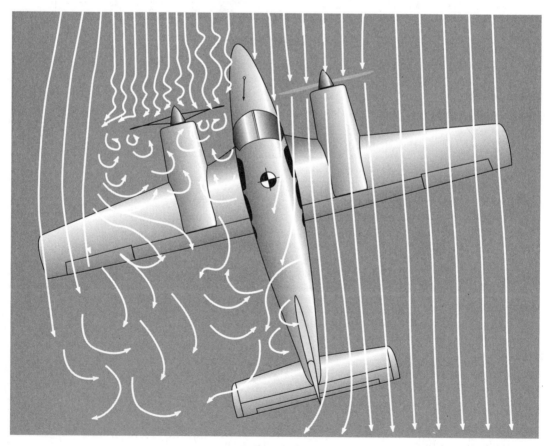

■ Engine failure

Application

■ **Engine Failure.**
- Indications of engine failure:
  - visual;
  - instrument.
- Control after engine failure:
  - yaw;
  - roll;
  - pitch.
- Identification of failed engine:
  - dead leg—dead engine;
  - confirmation.
- Engine failure in turns:
  - identification;
  - control.
- Alternative methods of control.

■ **Airspeed/power relationship.**
- Effect of varying speed at constant power.
- Effect of varying power at constant speed.

■ **Immediate actions in the event of engine failure.**

■ **Simulating engine failure.**
- Zero thrust:
  - definition;
  - purpose;
  - determination.
- Discuss feathering drill (including engine shutdown):
  - checklist procedures.
- Handling with one engine inoperative:
  - power required;
  - trim position for balanced flight;
  - flight controls positions for balanced flight.

■ **Fuel crossfeed.**

■ **Nursing a live engine.**

■ **Unfeather drill (airstart) checklist procedures.**

Conclusions (Summary and Review Questions)

Exercise F3
Introduction to Asymmetric Flight—Preflight Briefing

Aim

To teach the candidate safe control techniques in the event of engine failure. At the end of this flight the student should be able to handle the airplane confidently in asymmetric flight, and to understand engine failure, feathering and unfeathering drills (engine shutdown and airstart drills).

Air Exercise

- **Normal takeoff and climb.** *supervise*
- **Single-engine flight.**
  - Full feathering drill (engine shutdown). *demonstrate*
  - Checklist procedures.
- **Handling with one engine inoperative.**
  - Power required.
  - Trim position for balanced flight.
  - Flight controls positions for balanced flight.
  - Fuel crossfeed.
  - Unfeather drill (airstart). *demonstrate*
  - Checklist procedures.
  - Zero thrust condition.
  - Determination of "zero thrust" settings.
- **Simulated engine failure.**
  - Indications and symptoms of engine failure:
    - visual.
    - instrument; *demonstrate*
    - performance.
  - Control after engine failure:
    - yaw;
    - roll;
    - pitch.
  - Identification of failed engine.
- **Dead leg—dead engine.** *demonstrate, guide*
  - Instrument indications.
  - Alternative method of control.
- **Airspeed/power relationship.**
  - Effect of varying speed at constant power. *guide*
  - Effect of varying power at constant speed.
- **Practice handling in asymmetric flight.**

■ **Engine failure in turns.**
  • Identification;
  • Control.

Airmanship

■ **Decision point/speed.**
■ **Safety Brief.**
■ **V$_{MC}$ versus V$_S$.**
■ **Engine.** Minimum altitude for simulated engine failure and engine shutdown.
■ **Zero thrust procedure.**

Emergencies

■ **No unfeather.**

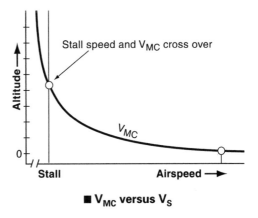

■ **V$_{MC}$ versus V$_S$**

Exercise F4
Minimum Control and Safety Speeds—Long Briefing

Objectives
At the end of the briefing the student will be able to describe the techniques for controlling the aircraft in asymmetric flight, discuss the pros and cons of each and state the relevant speeds for the aircraft type.

Introduction

Considerations
- **Review.** Previous flight and lessons.
- **Revision.** Engine failure—control and identification.

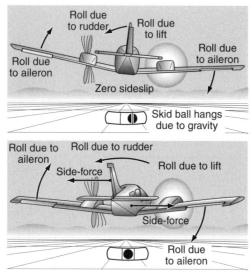

■ Angle of bank and wings level methods of control

Application
- **V**$_{MC}$.
  - Wings level method—windmilling engine.
  - Angle of bank method—windmilling engine.
  - Angle of bank method—zero thrust (= feathered propeller).

- **Engine failure during takeoff.** Below/at/above TOSS.
  - Full EFATO drill.
  - Single-engine climb.
- **Practice feathering and unfeathering drill.** Engine shutdown and airstart.

■ Asymmetric pattern, go-around and landing.

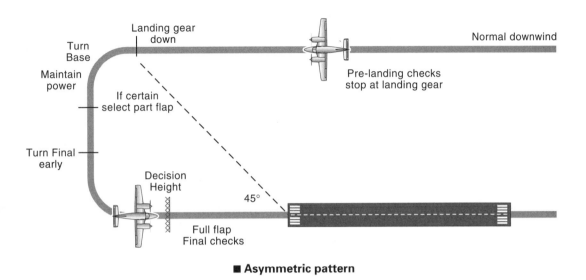

■ Asymmetric pattern

Conclusion (Summary and Review Questions)

Exercise F4
Minimum Control and Safety Speeds—Preflight Briefing

Aim

To investigate the significance of critical speeds and takeoff safety speed (TOSS or V_2). The candidate should understand the significance of critical speeds and takeoff safety speeds, should be able to handle an engine failure correctly in flight or during takeoff, and should be able to carry out feathering and unfeathering drills (shutdown and airstart) correctly.

Start/Taxi/Take-off

supervise

Climb/Transit

supervise

Air Exercise

■ **Revision**. Engine failure—control and identification.

■ **V$_{MC}$.**
  • Wings level method—windmilling engine.   *demonstrate, guide*
  • Angle of bank method—windmilling engine.
  • Angle of bank method—zero thrust.

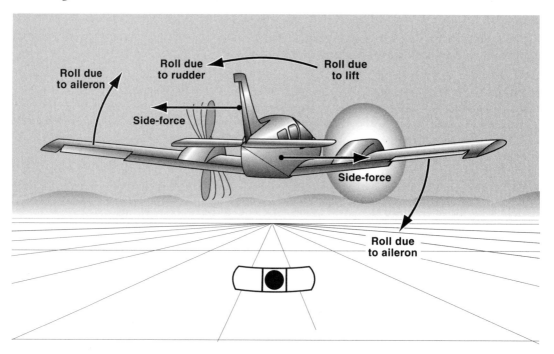

■ Wings level method of control

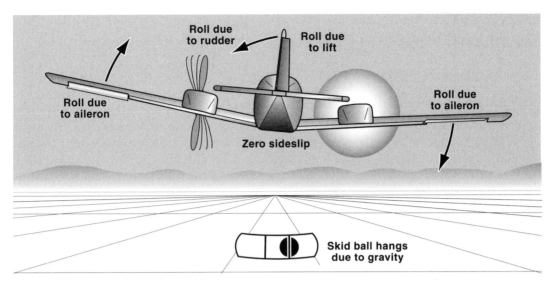

■ **Angle of Bank method of control**

■ **Engine failure during take-off.**
- Engine failure below TOSS.   *demonstrate*
- Engine failure at or above TOSS.
- Full EFATO drill.

■ **Single-engine climb.**

■ **Practice.** Feathering and unfeathering drill—engine shutdown and airstart.   *guide*

■ **Airplane handling.**

■ **Asymmetric patterns, go-around and landing.**   *demonstrate*

■ **Descent/approach and landing.**   *supervise*

Airmanship

■ *"Recover now"*—actions.

Emergencies

■ **Loss of control.**

Exercise F5
Asymmetric Patterns—Long Briefing

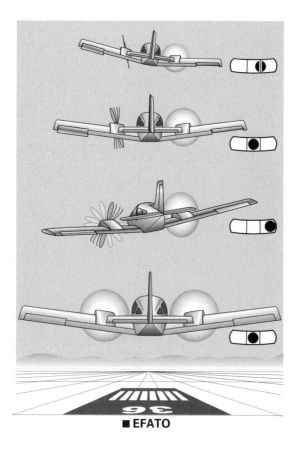

■ EFATO

Objectives

At the end of the briefing the student will be able to fully describe the asymmetric pattern including checks, settings, procedures and decision points.

Introduction

Considerations

■ **Control versus performance.**

Application

■ **Takeoff brief.**
■ **Engine failure after takeoff.**

■ **Asymmetric patterns.**
  • Attitudes, power settings and speeds.
  • Use of flap.
  • Landing gear and flap operation:
    • normal;
    • emergency.
  • Visual committal altitude:
    • consideration.
  • Go-around:
    • decision;
    • actions.

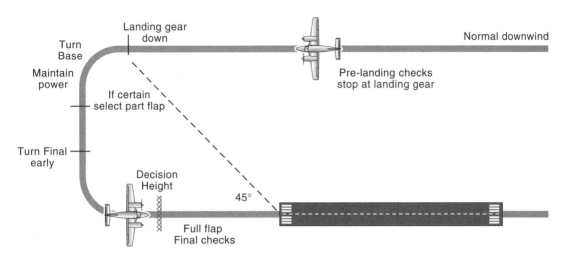

■ Asymmetric pattern

- Landing:
  - use of flap/decision height;
  - footload/trim;
  - taxiing.

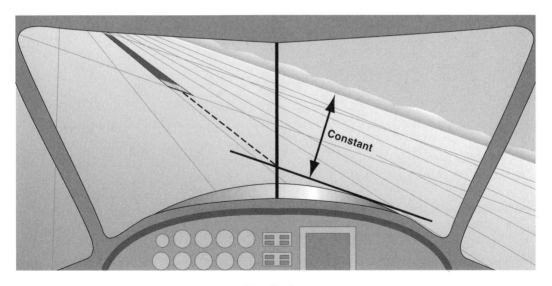

■ The final turn

Conclusion (Summary and Review Questions)

Exercise F5
Asymmetric Patterns—Preflight Briefing

Aim of the Flight
The candidate will be able to handle an engine failure after takeoff, and to safely carry out an asymmetric pattern, go-around and landing. The candidate should be able to demonstrate an ability to handle an engine failure after takeoff and to carry out an asymmetric pattern and land safely and competently at the flight test standard, i.e. maintain selected speeds within 5 knots and headings within 10° during simulated engine failure operations.

Air Exercise
- **Takeoff brief.**
- **Engine failure after takeoff.**   *guide*
- **Asymmetric pattern.**

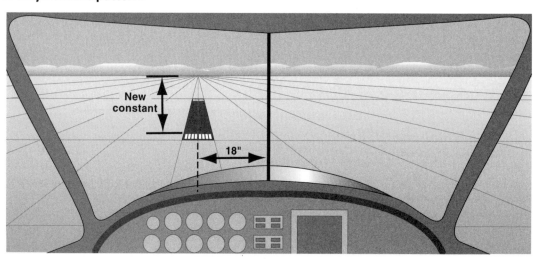

■ Stabilized approach—Decision? Land or go-around

- Power settings and speeds.
- Use of flap.
- Landing gear and flap operation:
  - normal;
  - emergency.   *guide*
- Visual committal altitude:
  - consideration.   *guide*
- Go-around:
  - decision;   *guide*
  - actions.

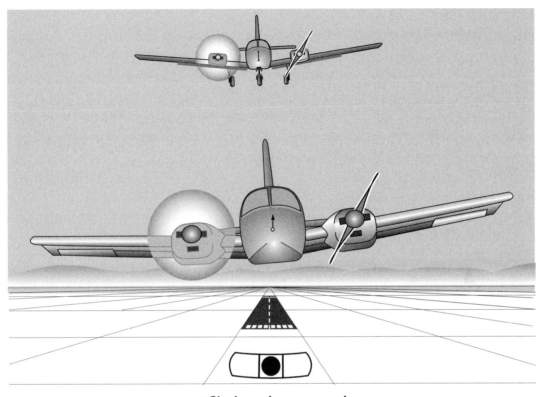

■ Single-engine go-around

- Landing;
  - use of flap;
  - footload;
  - taxiing.

guide

Airmanship

- ■ *"I have control"/ "you have control"*.
- ■ **Setting zero thrust.**
- ■ **ATC notification of practice asymmetric.**

Emergencies

- ■ **Obstructed runway, short final.**

Exercise F6
Asymmetric Performance and Pattern—Long Briefing

Objectives
At the end of the briefing the student will be able to state the effect on aircraft and system performance as a result of engine failure. He will be able to describe the pattern, procedures, checks, attitudes and power settings for a practice asymmetric pattern.

Introduction

Considerations
Review of previous lessons.

Application
- **Effect on aircraft systems.**
  - Engine parameters.
  - Electrical system operation.
  - Hydraulic system operation.
  - Fuel system:
    - crossfeed;
    - fuel consumption.
  - Other systems—type related.
- **Effect on performance.**
  - Feathering.
  - Configuration (e.g. flaps, landing gear).
  - Departure from scheduled speeds.
- **Effect on climb/cruise performance.**
  - Climb.
  - Range.
  - Endurance.
  - Descent.
- **Asymmetric patterns.**

Conclusions (Summary and Review Questions)

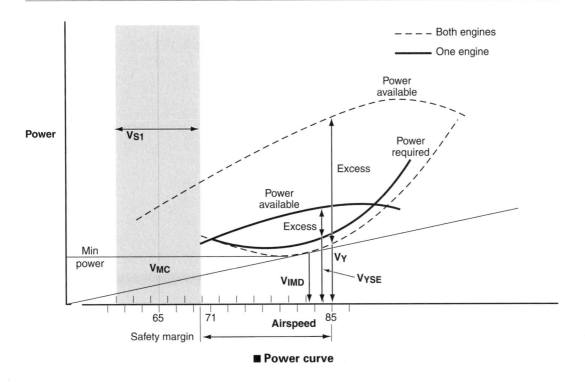

■ Power curve

Exercise F6
Asymmetric Performance and Pattern—Preflight Briefing

Aim of the Flight
The student will be able to state the effects of asymmetric operation on airplane systems and performance, and after practice, consistently complete asymmetric patterns.

Air Exercise
■ **Effect on aircraft systems.**
  - Engine parameters;
  - Electrical system operation. *demonstrate*
  - Hydraulic system operation. *demonstrate*
  - Fuel system.
  - Crossfeed: *demonstrate*
    - fuel consumption;
    - other systems—type related.
■ **Effect on performance.**
  - Feathering. *guide*
  - Configuration (e.g. flaps, landing gear). *guide*
  - Departure from scheduled speeds. *guide*
■ **Effect on climb/cruise performance.**
  - Climb.
  - Range.
  - Endurance. *guide*
  - Descent.
■ **Asymmetric patterns.** *guide*

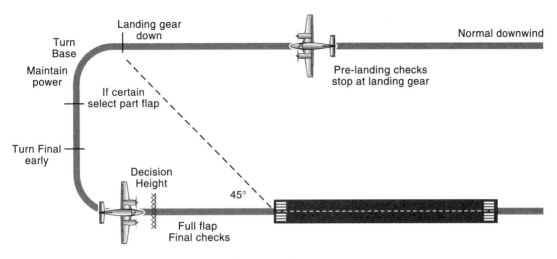

■ Asymmetric pattern

Airmanship

- **Simulated feather.** Zero thrust.
- **Minimum altitude.** Feathered engine.

Emergencies

Exercise F7
Instrument Flying—Long Briefing

Objectives
At the end of the briefing the student will be able to control the aircraft safely under normal and asymmetric conditions with reference to the flight instruments.

Introduction
- **Review.** Instrument flying.

Considerations
- **Selective radial scan.**
- **Physiological factors.**

Application
- **Normal flight** (all engines operative).
  - Straight and level.
  - Climbing and descending (attitudes and power settings).
  - Turning.
  - Unusual attitude recoveries.
- **Asymmetric flight** (one engine inoperative).
  - Engine failure:
    - identification and control.
  - Straight and level.
  - Climbing and descending.
  - Turning.
  - Effect of flap and/or landing gear.
- **Asymmetric instrument approach and circle to landing.**
- **Asymmetric ILS.**

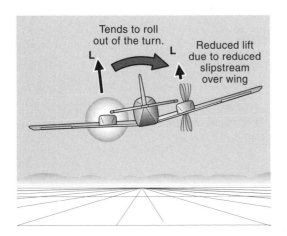

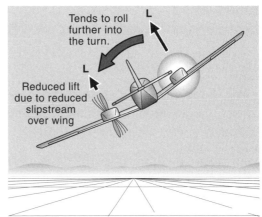

■ Engine failure during a gentle turn

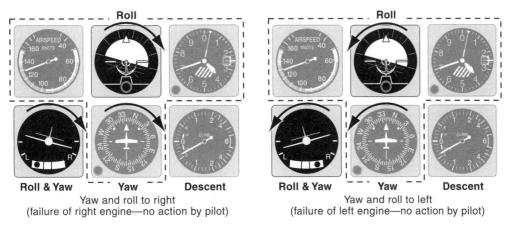

Yaw and roll to right
(failure of right engine—no action by pilot)

Yaw and roll to left
(failure of left engine—no action by pilot)

■ Instrument trends

Conclusions (Summary and Review Questions)

Exercise F7
Instrument Flying—Preflight Briefing

Aim

At the completion of the flight the candidate will be able to complete an instrument flight in normal conditions, control, identify and secure a failed engine and complete an instrument approach including a circling visual approach.

Skill Standard

The candidate should be able to control the airplane and its systems in instrument flight conditions with one engine inoperative:

Air Exercise

- **Start, taxi, takeoff.**
- **Normal flight** (all engines operative).   *supervise*
  - Straight and level.
  - Climbing and descending.
  - Turning.
  - Unusual attitude recovery.   *guide*
- **Asymmetric flight** (one engine inoperative).   *guide*
  - Engine failure:
    - identification and control;
  - Straight and level.
  - Climbing and descending.
  - Turning.   *supervise*
  - Effect of flap and/or landing gear.
- **Asymmetric instrument approach and circle to landing.**   *demonstrate*
- **Asymmetric ILS.**   *guide*

Airmanship

- V_{MC} versus V_{STALL}.

Emergencies

- **Loss of control.**

Exercise F8
Night Asymmetric Patterns—Long Briefing

Objectives

Introduction

Considerations
- **Physiological factors.**

Application
- **Takeoff brief.**
- **Takeoff, normal pattern and landing.**
- **Engine Failure after takeoff.**
- **Asymmetric pattern.**

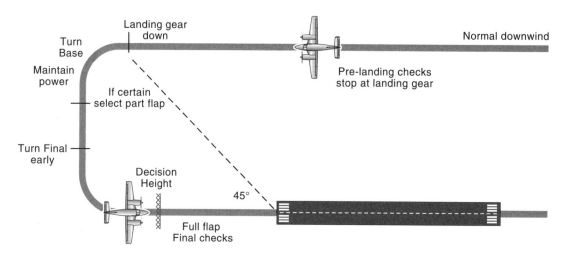

■ Asymmetric Pattern

■ **Asymmetric go-around.**

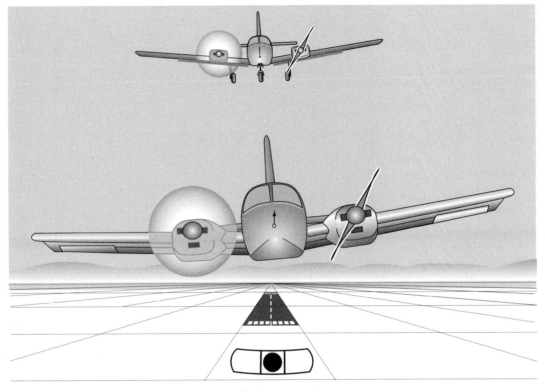

■ **Going around**

■ **Asymmetric landing.**

Conclusion (Summary and Review Questions)

Exercise F8
Night Asymmetric Patterns—Preflight Briefing

Aim
At the end of the flight the candidate will be able to safely fly asymmetric patterns at night.

Skill Standard
The candidate should be able to carry out the air exercises at night safely and correctly.

Air Exercise
- **Takeoff brief.**
- **Takeoff, normal pattern and landing.**
- **Local procedures.**
- **Radio calls.**
- **Engine failure after takeoff.**
- **Asymmetric pattern.**
- **Asymmetric go-around.**
- **Asymmetric landing.**

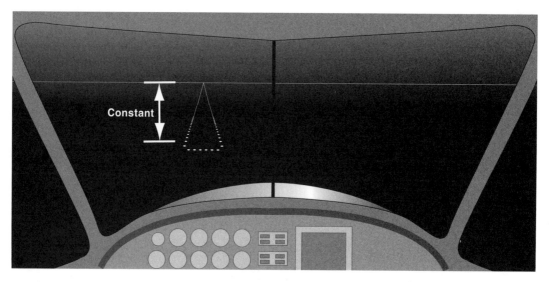

■ The runway edges converge at the horizon

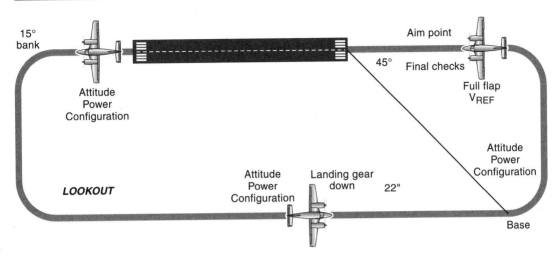

■ **Pattern diagram**

Airmanship
- **Night sight.**
- **Flashlights.**
- **Decision height.**
- **Local procedures.**

Emergencies
- **Landing light failure.**
- **Radio failure.**
- **Light signals.**

Radio Failure	
Try other mike/headset Squawk 7600 Listen to NDB	
Light Signals	
Steady Green	Clear to Land
Steady Red	Continue Circling
Flashing Green	Return for Landing
Flashing Red	Do Not Land

■ **No radio procedure/signals**

Chapter 11

Questions you must and questions you should be able to answer about your aircraft

Introduction

The following is information you should know or be able to find readily before you fly your twin alone.

General Aircraft Data

1. What is the make, type and model of the airplane?
2. In which category (categories) is the airplane permitted to fly?

Airspeed Limitations

1. List the applicable airspeed for the airplane type:
   (a) V_{NO}
   (b) V_{NE}
   (c) maximum demonstrated crosswind
   (d) V_A (design maneuver speed)
   (e) V_X, V_{XSE}
   (f) Turbulence penetration speed
   (g) V_{S1}
   (h) V_{SO}
   (i) V_Y, V_{YSE}
   (j) V_{FE} (takeoff flap)
   (k) V_{FE} (full flap)
   (l) V_{LO1} (ldg gear operation up)
   (m) V_{LE} (ldg gear extended)
   (n) V_{LO2} (ldg gear operating)
   (o) V_{MC}
   (p) V_{SSE}
   (q) V_{REF} (max landing weight)
   (r) maximum landing light operating speed (if applicable);
   (s) maximum load factor (flaps up) is + ____ g and − ____ g.

Emergency Procedures

1. Detail the emergency procedures for the following situations:
   (a) engine fire on the ground;
   (b) engine failure on takeoff;
   - before decision point;
   - after decision point;
   (c) engine fire in flight;
   (d) engine failure in the cruise;
   (e) electrical fire on the ground;
   (f) electrical fire in flight;
   (g) cabin fire in flight;
   (h) rapid depressurization;
   (i) waste gate failure;
   (j) emergency landing gear extension procedure;
   (k) propeller overspeed;
   (l) cockpit lighting failure.

Normal Procedures

1. State, describe or detail:
   (a) the start sequence for cold and hot starts;
   (b) the RPM used for run-up checks;
   (c) the feathering system (if applicable);
   (d) minimum RPM for feathering;
   (e) the ignition system;
   (f) use of the carburetor heat (company SOPs);
   (g) the maximum RPM drop and RPM differential between magnetos;
   (h) the use of cowl flaps;
   (i) the climb attitude, power setting, IAS and fuel flow;
   (j) a typical 65% power setting, IAS and fuel flow at 5,000 ft pressure altitude;
   (k) using the airplane flight manual, calculate the endurance for the airplane at 5,000 ft MSL (ISA) with 65% power set; and
   (l) how the mixtures are leaned in the cruise.

Weight and Balance and Performance

1. Specify the correct values of:
   (a) the maximum ramp weight;
   (b) the maximum takeoff weight;

(c) the maximum landing weight;

(d) the maximum zero fuel weight;

(e) the maximum number of adult persons on board (POB);

(f) the maximum baggage weight;

(g) the maximum fuel which can be carried with a full load of adult passengers (170 lb/person) and maximum baggage weight.

2. Do any of the weight limitations in (a) to (g) vary between categories? If so, what are the weight limitations of each category?

3. Using the airplane flight manual, at a typical loading determine the takeoff weight and balance solution (maximum takeoff weight and CG position), the amount of fuel that can be carried, and the endurance:

(a) Calculate the takeoff distance required at maximum takeoff weight, 2,500 ft MSL and OAT 30°C, and the landing distance at maximum landing weight.

(b) Calculate single-engine climb rate and gradient under the above conditions.

(c) Discuss the pros and cons of factoring the takeoff and landing distances.

Fuel System, Fuel and Fluids

1. State, sketch or show on the aircraft diagram:

(a) the correct grade of fuel;

(b) any approved alternate fuel;

(c) the location of fuel tanks and drain points;

(d) the total and usable fuel in each tank;

(e) the position of the fuel tank vents;

(f) when refuelling to less than full tanks, what restrictions apply, and how is the fuel quantity checked;

(g) describe the priming system and its use;

(h) where the fuel boost/auxiliary pumps are located;

(i) are these electrical or mechanical?

(j) when pumps should be used;

(k) the fuel tank selection and balance procedure;

(l) the conditions applying to tank selection for takeoff and landing;

(m) if applicable, describe the crossfeed system;

(n) if applicable, the minimum and normal hydraulic fluid capacity;

(o) the correct grade of oil for the airplane;

(p) the minimum oil quantity before flight;

(q) the maximum quantity of oil;

(r) the maximum, minimum and normal engine oil pressures; and

(s) the maximum, minimum and normal engine oil temperatures.

Asymmetric Performance

Answer the following questions:
1. What IAS is V_{MC} in the takeoff configuration?
2. What effect will full flap have on V_{MC}?
3. What is the fuel flow rate with one engine shut down at 1,000 ft MSL on an ISA day?
4. What is the rate of climb with one engine shut down, propeller feathered, max gross weight, 1,000 ft MSL, takeoff power, landing gear and flap retracted;
   (a) on an ISA day?
   (b) on an ISA = 20 day?
5. Which engine is the critical engine?
6. What is the single-engine climb speed (V_{YSE})?
7. How does single-engine flight affect the range of the airplane?

Engine and Propeller
1. What is the make/model of the engines?
2. What is the power output, and number of cylinders?
3. What is the takeoff power setting and time limit?
4. What is the maximum continuous power?
5. Are the engines fuel injected or normally aspirated?
6. Are the engines supercharged or turbocharged?
7. What is the maximum MP permitted?
8. If turbocharged, what:
   (a) is the type of waste gate fitted (fixed, manual or automatic)?
   (b) is the procedure for operating the wastegate?
   (c) prevents the engine from being overboosted?
9. If supercharged, what:
   (a) prevents the engine from being overboosted?
   (b) controls the MP in the climb/descent?
10. Describe the propeller governing system; and
11. If the oil pressure to the propeller is lost, does the propeller go into coarse or fine pitch?
12. What is the zero thrust setting?
13. What is the propeller unfeathering/engine restart procedure?

Airframe

1. What type is the landing gear system (fixed/retractable/tricycle/conventional)?
2. Describe the trim system.
3. Describe the flap actuating system and indicating system.

4. What is the flap operating range and airspeed limits?
5. Sketch the location of all exits and describe their operation.
6. What is the wing span of the airplane?

Auxiliary Systems

Answer the following questions:
1. What systems are hydraulically operated?
2. How many brake applications would be expected from a fully pressurized brake accumulator (if applicable)?
3. What are the sources of electrical power?
4. What is the DC system voltage?
5. Can an external power source be used?
   (a) If so, what is the procedure?
   (b) Where are the battery and external power receptacle located?
6. How long can the battery supply emergency power?
7. Following an alternator/generator failure in flight, which non-essential electrical services should be switched off?
8. Which, if any, auxiliary system(s) will be lost if the left engine was shut down and the propeller feathered?
9. Which, if any, auxiliary system(s) will be lost if the right engine was shut down and the propeller feathered?
10. If a stall warning device is fitted, is it electrical or mechanical?
11. How is the cockpit ventilated?
12. How is the cockpit heated?
13. If a fuel burning heater is installed, describe the method used to turn the heater on and off and detail any limitations.
14. What is the fuel consumption of the heater?
15. Describe the pressurization system (if applicable).
16. Show the location of the following safety equipment:
    (a) fire extinguisher;
    (b) ELT;
    (c) flashlights;
    (d) survival equipment; and
    (e) first aid kit.

Flight Instruments

1. Where are the pitot head(s), static vent(s) and any water drain points for the pitot/static system located?
2. Is there a pitot heat system fitted?

3. Is there an alternate static source fitted? If so:
    (a) where is this located?
    (b) What is the purpose of this system?
    (c) If used, what effect does it have on the pressure instruments?
4. Which flight instruments are operated electrically?
5. Which flight instruments are gyroscopically operated?
6. Which instruments are operated by vacuum?

Piloting

General Handling

Complete the attitude, power and performance table for your aircraft.

Patterns

Complete a pattern diagram (AEO and OEI) for your aircraft with attitude, power setting, speeds, checks and decision points.

Stall, Spin, Unusual Attitude Recovery

Describe the stall, spin and UA recovery technique for your aircraft.

***

Afterword

It is our sincere hope that armed with the knowledge you have gained from this book, together with the practical training and briefings from your instructor, you will be well prepared for a safe and enjoyable future as a multi-engine pilot. *May the thrust be with you*—at least until above V_{YSE}.

Next step, turbines!

Happy takeoffs.